The Possibility of
Weakness of Will

Publication of this work has been supported
by the National Endowment for the Humanities,
a federal agency that supports the study of fields such as
history, philosophy, literature, and languages.

Winner of the 1984 Johnsonian Prize

The Possibility of
Weakness of Will

ROBERT DUNN

Hackett Publishing Company
INDIANAPOLIS

Cover design by Jackie Lacy
Interior design by J. M. Matthew

For further information, please address

Hackett Publishing Company
P.O. Box 44937
Indianapolis, Ind. 46204

Library of Congress Cataloging-in-Publication Data

Dunn, Robert, b. 1949.
    The possibility of weakness of will.

    Bibliography: p.
    Includes index.
    1. Will. 2. Ethics. I. Title.
BJ1468.5.D85   1986   128'.3   87-24784
ISBN 0-915145-99-5
ISBN 0-915145-98-7 (pbk.)

For William Hurley

Contents

Acknowledgements

SEVERAL PHILOSOPHERS have helped me to improve this essay. I should like to thank especially Les Holborow, Don Mannison, Alan White, Michael Stocker, Lloyd Reinhardt, Michael Carey, Ian Hinckfuss, André Gallois, and the editors, readers, and editorial staff of the *Journal of Philosophy*.

Les Holborow and Don Mannison carefully supervised an earlier version that I submitted as my doctoral dissertation to the Department of Philosophy at the University of Queensland in June 1983. Alan White, Michael Stocker, and Lloyd Reinhardt commented on this version as examiners. Michael Carey first got me interested in the topic, and he and I spent many a pleasant evening in Brisbane at Lucky's Trattoria eating chicken cacciatora and discussing weakness of will and related issues. Ian Hinckfuss was unfailingly supportive during the time I was writing my dissertation, and, indeed, it was he who bullied me into trying for the Johnsonian Prize. André Gallois was a constant source of challenge to my thinking. One of the subtlest thinkers I know, André was irrepressible in arguing the case against me with immense vigour and ingenuity. In this way I was often alerted to the full complexity of the issues with which I was trying to deal.

Winning the Johnsonian Prize earned me a rare privilege. I now had the opportunity to work the essay into publishable shape under the expert guidance of the editors, readers, and editorial staff of the *Journal of Philosophy*. I learned much from this exercise, and the result, for all its remaining blemishes—for which I must claim total responsibility—is a much better piece, in both style and substance.

I also owe a debt of thanks to an old and dear friend of mine, Geraldine Suter, for preparing the index. I knew when Geraldine agreed to do this for me that I would end up with an index that would be the envy of many an author.

There are two other people I should like to thank, last but not least. They are James Moore and William Hurley. I met Jim in the final year of writing my dissertation, and his friendship and enthusiasm for philosophy made the difference when spirits were very low. As for Bill, he is a psychiatrist friend of mine who, from beginning to end, encouraged me in the present project, and whose own views on relevant matters, coming from a quite different perspective, have always given me much to think about. It is to him that I have dedicated this book.

Sydney   R. D.
August 1986

CHAPTER ONE

The Possibility Of
Weakness Of Will

IS IT POSSIBLE for an agent to be weak-willed in what he does? That
is to say, can an agent knowingly and intentionally act against his
full-fledged all-out summary better judgement,[1] or judgement
about what is right, or some such, when he is free to act in accordance with it, has the relevant know-how, and has present to
mind the judgement that now is the time to act? Apparently so.
Pre-reflectively, such weakness of will would seem a familiar,
everyday phenomenon. And yet some philosophers, ancient and
contemporary, have considered the possibility of such weakness
problematic. For on their view, typically, such all-out summary
evaluation about action as characterizes the putative weak-willed
agent is connected with desire, or choice, or intention, or some
such volitional thinking, and the latter, in turn, is connected with
action, in ways that conflict with the possibility of weakness of will
so understood, or, as it is often also called, incontinence, or
akrasia.

I

Plato is a case in point. On Plato's interpretation in *The Protagoras*, the so-called weak-willed agent, or *akrates*, is typified by
Milton's Eve, who is misled by Satan, and not by Adam, who
follows Eve "against his better knowledge."[2] For apparent cases
of weakness, Socrates argues in *The Protagoras*, really are cases of
ignorance: a failure of cognition or intellect (357d–e, 358c). In particular, the agent misestimates what is best, that is, most

1

pleasant,[3] because of the nearness in time of a certain pleasure (355–358). What is here critical for Plato's Socrates is the idea that desire or choice aligns itself with all-out summary evaluation about action.[4] In putative cases of weakness we are required to suppose, *per impossibile,* that these two come apart, and that an agent, while knowing or believing[5] that an action is less than the best, that is, most pleasant, nonetheless desires or chooses to do it and does it (351b–358d).

The later Plato, it is worth remarking, develops a psychology that allows for action contrary to all-out summary evaluation.[6] For, in addition to the desires of reason, Plato comes to acknowledge the independent desires of appetite and of spirit or passion, in accord with his tripartite division of the mind into reason, appetite, and spirit or passion (*Republic,* 439–40; 580–81), and to accept that persons can act from appetite or passion contrary to their all-out summary evaluations. At this point, however, it becomes an issue whether such actions count for Plato as akratic. For, insofar as they do, akratic action so conceived differs from putative weak-willed action. For one thing, such actions against all-out summary evaluations are not clearly, at the time of their performance, knowingly done as such; and secondly, the relevant "agents" are depicted by Plato as slaves "under the mad tyranny" of over-powering and unreasoning (*Republic,* 437–38; 441) desires (*Republic,* 577–78; 588–90). Witness the plight of Alcibiades: in the presence of Socrates he clearly knows that Socrates is right about how best to live, but, corrupted in nature, when he is away from Socrates he loses sight of what he knows and its particular consequences, acting then from appetite and ambition (*Republic,* 494–95; *Symposium,* 214e ff).

It is interesting to compare Aristotle with Plato. For in the *Nicomachean Ethics,* book 7, akrasia is interpreted as, at heart, ignorance—a failure of cognition or intellect. Indeed, Aristotle's interpretation of akrasia is reminiscent in *some* degree of the later Plato, although in canvassing the contentious issues Aristotle addresses himself only to Plato's Socrates of *The Protagoras* (1145b; 1147b). For Aristotle there is a problem about the possibility of akrasia or incontinence because of the way in which, in the putative akrates' practical reasoning, ratiocinative desire or choice, characteristically the efficient cause of action, aligns itself with his all-out summary evaluation about action (1139a–b; Fourth Solution, 1147a).[7]

According to Aristotle, the sphere of akrasia proper corresponds to that of self-indulgence or intemperance, namely, the pleasures of touch and taste (1117b–19a; 1147–48b2). Self-indulgence, however, is vice; and the self-indulgent agent, in pursuing the pleasures of touch or taste, acts from conviction and choice. Akrasia or incontinence, by contrast, is not vice, at least not strictly; and the incontinent agent, in going for the pleasures of touch or taste, acts contrary to conviction and choice. Although, like the self-indulgent agent, he does wrong, the incontinent agent is like the morally virtuous (1098a; 1103a ff; 1178a) temperate (1117b ff) agent, and unlike the wicked self-indulgent one, in that he acknowledges the right rule about what is good for him with respect to the pleasures of touch and taste, namely, that one should live temperately (1148a3; 1150b–52a). The akrates, however, falls short of possessing practical wisdom such as is characteristic of the morally virtuous agent, that is, knowledge about what in general is good for one, which is indefeasibly efficacious, given relevant supplementary knowledge about particulars (1140a–b; 1141b ff; 1146a; 1152a; 1178a).

There are, in fact, in Aristotle's scheme, two sorts of akrasia: weakness and impetuosity—"Some men deliberate and then, because of their feelings, cannot stand by the course they have determined upon; others do not stay to deliberate, and are consequently led by their feelings" (1150b). The impetuous akrates clearly is incontinent in ignorance of what he should do, or is right, in the particular circumstance. The situation of the so-called weak akrates is less perspicuous. For although, as we have just seen, Aristotle in some passages characterizes him as someone who reaches an evaluative conclusion and choice for his particular circumstance, elsewhere (Fourth Solution, 1147a–b) he apparently characterizes him as someone who, at least at the time of action, is ignorant of how he should act, or of what is right, in the particular circumstance. For Aristotle, it seems, the weak akrates concludes what he should do, or is right, in the particular circumstance, but, under the influence of appetite or passion, temporarily has only impaired knowledge of this: knows this only in an attenuated sense.[8]

It is noteworthy that limitations attach to incontinent or akratic action proper, as Aristotle conceives matters, which do not in the least attach to putative weakness of will, as conceived in the terms of my original question.[9] For example, such akrasia typically involves evaluative *knowledge* or *correct* opinion (*right* reason) and countervailing *wrongful* desire.[10] Also such akrasia concerns actions done from certain sensual desires, namely, desires for the pleasures of touch or taste. No such circumscriptions attach to putative weakness of will. Donleavy's Samuel S. ("Saint Stubborn Sam of the Sealed Lips and Crazy Celibacy"), who wants so much, but contrary to his (curious) better judgement, to have a quick tumble with Abigail, would be a candidate for weakness were he to yield to Abigail's wiles[11]; and equally would a faltering Genet who, like Milton's Satan,[12] (perversely) thinks it best to perpetrate morally evil acts, but who, unlike Satan, finds this difficult in the face of a passionate attachment to doing what he judges morally good.[13] Interestingly, Aristotle himself distinguishes between qualified and unqualified akrasia.[14] Agents who act incontinently from desires for the pleasures of touch or taste are simply or unqualifiedly akratic; whereas those who act incontinently from desires for the pleasures of victory, honour, wealth, etc., or from a passion like anger, are qualifiedly akratic (1147b–48b2). According to Aristotle, incontinence of anger is preferable to that of the appetites (1149a–1149b).[15]

In any case, however, incontinent or akratic action, as finally countenanced by Aristotle, falls outside the scope of such putative weakness of will as concerns me. Three reasons for this are as follows. First, such action is not a clear case of knowingly going against one's better knowledge or judgement, or knowledge or judgement about what is right, and so on. For Aristotle's akrates does not act in the *full and conscious* knowledge or belief that, in the particular circumstance, he should do otherwise. Second, Aristotle's akrates is hardly free to do as he, albeit in a mitigated sense, knows or thinks he should, or is right. For he characteristically acts in the grip of overpowering feelings. Of course, Aristotle himself would deny that the akrates acts under compulsion: the appetite or passion from which he acts is *in him*, and, according to

Aristotle, "those things of which the moving principle is in a man himself are in his power to do or not to do" (1110a–b9). But this is entirely unconvincing. Finally, there is a problem about classifying akratic action, as Aristotle conceives it, as intentional. For Aristotle does not operate with any clear notion of intention. At one place in the *Nicomachean Ethics* (1142b), in connection, indeed, with incontinence, he apparently employs a concept very like the concept of bare intention, in relation to calculative reasoning that is split off from an agent's ulterior desire (rational wish) for his own good (1111b; 1113a), but Aristotle nowhere pays attention to this concept in his account of action. Instead he focuses on *choice* or *prohairesis* which, construed as desire resulting from deliberation about how to act for one's own good, is indissolubly tied to an agent's ultimate rational wish for his *summum bonum* (1111b–13a; 1139a–b).[16]

To conclude, neither Plato nor Aristotle allows that weakness of will, as conceived in the terms of my original question, is possible. For both, what is crucial is a claimed relation between the all-out summary evaluation about action the supposed weak-willed agent makes, which they identify as *prudential* evaluation, and desire or choice on his part. But there is nothing persuasive about this classical version of a relation between such evaluative and volitional thinking. In the first place, all-out summary evaluation about action need not be, or correspond to, prudential evaluation. In the second, what in this picture at base explains the claimed connection between all-out summary evaluative and volitional thinking is the presence in an agent of a prior ulterior desire for his own good.[17] But, quite simply, the presence in an agent of such an anterior volition is not in any way guaranteed. To state a theme I develop in Chapter 5, persons perfectly well can be in moods or, more generally, frames or sets of mind, on account of which they are indifferent, or even hostile, toward themselves.

II

The question of whether weakness of will is possible was vigorously revived by R. M. Hare in *The Language of Morals* (*LM*, 1952) and *Freedom and Reason* (*FR*, 1963). For Hare, very clearly, the problem about the possibility of weakness arises out of the combination of two theses, one which relates the putative weak-willed agent's all-out summary evaluation about action[18] to volitional thinking, and a second which relates volitional thinking to (intentional) action. For Hare these alignments between evaluation and the will, and the will and intentional action, obtain as matters of *logical* necessity. Plato and Aristotle, it is noteworthy, are less perspicuous on this point.[19]

In *LM* at 11.2, Hare advances the following test for whether someone who judges that he ought to do something *x* is really making a value judgement:

> . . . the test, whether someone is using the judgement 'I ought to do X' as a value-judgement or not is, 'Does he or does he not recognise that if he assents to the judgement, he must also assent to the command "Let me do X"?' (*LM* 11.2, pp. 168–69).

This test encapsulates the semantic thesis that genuine evaluative terms, as opposed to their "inverted commas" counterparts (*LM* 7.5, pp. 124–25; 11.1–.2), introduce into judgements like "I ought to do *x*", in addition to descriptive meaning (*LM* 7; *FR* 2.6–.8), imperative or prescriptive meaning, at the level of full universal prescriptiveness,[20] with the result that such judgements are action-guiding, that is, answers to practical questions of what to do (*LM* 2.5, p. 29; 3.4, p. 46; 5.11). Earlier in *LM*, at 2.2, Hare also proposes:

> It is a tautology to say that we cannot sincerely assent to a command addressed to ourselves, and *at the same time* not perform it, if now is the occasion for performing it, and it is in our (physical and psychological) power to do so (*LM*, 2.2, p. 20; *FR* 5.7, p. 79).[21]

The idea here is that the sincere assent in question corresponds to a resolve or intention to act, the content of which is expressible in words in the first-person singular imperative (*LM* 2.2, pp. 19–20; *FR* 4.3, pp. 54–55). For Hare, it is in light of these two com-

mitments, one of which connects evaluative with volitional thinking and the other of which connects volitional thinking with
(intentional) action, that the

> familiar 'Socratic' paradox arises, in that it becomes analytic
> to say that everyone always does what he thinks he ought to
> (in the evaluative sense) [to which, in a footnote, he ap-
> pends the qualification: "Strictly, 'always, if physically and
> psychologically able' " (*LM* 11.2, p. 169).]

In *LM* Hare registers his dissatisfaction with his commitment
to the so-called Socratic paradox. This does not accord with how
we use the word *think*, he comments: "The trouble arises because
our criteria, in ordinary speech, for saying 'He thinks he ought'
are exceedingly elastic. If a person does not do something, but the
omission is accompanied by feelings of guilt, etc., we normally say
that he has not done what he thinks he ought" (*LM* 11.2, p. 169).
Hare then proceeds to foreshadow a way out for himself: "It is
therefore necessary to qualify the criterion given above for
'sincerely assenting to a command', and to admit that there are
degrees of sincere assent, not all of which involve actually obeying
the command" (*LM* 11.2, pp. 169–70).
Hare's mature consideration of the possibility of weakness of
will appears in *FR*. What now emerges as analytic is something of
this order:

> If an agent N judges that he ought to do x, as a matter of full
> assent and with a "full-blooded" (that is, universally
> prescriptive) employment of *ought*, thinks that now is the
> time to act, and has present to mind both the judgement that
> he ought and the thought that now is the time, N will do x
> (intentionally), provided that he is physically and
> psychologically able so to act and has the relevant know-
> how.[22]

The idea here is that the imperative or prescriptive ingredient in
evaluative thinking—or better, its expression in language—ties
such thinking constitutively to desire or wanting (*FR* 9.4, pp.

167–70), and that, in the case in question, N's all-out summary evaluative thinking will incorporate, specifically, an *intention* to act (full assent to a first-person singular imperative)[23] whose execution is logically assured.

Hare's strategy in *FR* is to make logical room for weakness of will in the light of this refined view of what is analytic. The new picture is that weakness assumes various forms, although, typically, weak-willed agents are *psychologically powerless* to do as they think they should (*FR* 5.7–.9, pp. 77 ff). Picking up on his remarks about degrees of assent in *LM*, Hare now explicitly requires—if there is to be a problem about weakness—that a universally prescriptive evaluation be a case of *full* assent. For only in such a case does an agent, in making an evaluative judgement, form a volition that is an *intention* or *commitment* to act (*FR* 5.6, p. 76, lines 25–26; 5.9, p. 83, lines 20 ff). Hare's special focus, however, is on weakness that (according to him) exploits the semantics of human evaluative language in its special pleading uses. If N's judgement that he ought to do x is genuinely evaluative, the story goes, it (or, better, its expression in language) will include imperative or prescriptive meaning. This element in its meaning, however, has the potentiality to be downgraded from full universal prescriptivity; and, in cases of special pleading, agents trade on this. N's judgement about what he ought to do, in such a case, falls short of full universal prescriptivity *in his own favour*: N wills (prescribes) that certain others should do x in circumstances relevantly like his own, but exempts himself, thus failing, in such willing, to form a volition to do x in his particular circumstance (*FR* 4.3, pp. 52–53; 5.5–.6, pp. 73–77; 5.8, pp. 81–82).[24]

Hare's concessions to weakness stem from a position which remains inhospitable to the logical possibility of such weakness of will as concerns me. Furthermore, Hare's recasting of weakness as typically involving psychological inability is entirely counterintuitive. For weakness, it seems, *contrasts* with such powerlessness as an explanation of a hiatus between an agent's all-out summary evaluation about action and what he does. What Hare seems to be suggesting is that the hiatus occurs because the agent *lacks* the requisite will power or self-control, that is, the capacity to counteract such motivational influences as are at odds with his all-out summary evaluation about action—the capacity to act in accordance with his all-out summary evaluation *despite* such contrary influences.[25] He acts, in short, from irresistible disinclining desire. What calling an agent *weak-willed* suggests, by contrast, it would appear, is that the breach between evaluation and action exists because, although the agent *possesses* the requisite will power or self-control, he fails to make the effort of will that would be its exercise; he yields or gives in to countervailing desire. In *Seize the Day*, Saul Bellow tells us that ten decisions against his better judgement make up the history of Tommy Wilhelm's life (pp. 26–27 et passim). But we do not understand Wilhelm, I would contend, if we think him weak-willed. His predicament is something else: a chronically crippling *absence* of self-restraint. In the confusion of powerlessness with weakness, one is reminded of John Austin's remark in "A Plea for Excuses": "Or we collapse succumbing to temptation into losing control of ourselves—a bad patch, this, for telescoping".[26] Aquinas was sensitive to what is at issue here. In the *Summa Theologiae* (at Q156, article 2), he concludes, "In the incontinent rational judgement is overwhelmed, not of necessity . . . but through some negligence in resisting passion by holding firm to reason".[27]

III

Another contemporary philosopher who has been troubled by the claim that there are weak-willed or incontinent actions is Donald Davidson. In his paper, "How is Weakness of the Will Possible?" (*EAE*, pp. 21–42), Davidson's preferred characterization of weakness or incontinence is in these terms:

> D. In doing x an agent acts incontinently if and only if (a) the agent does x intentionally; (b) the agent believes there is an alternative action y open to him; and (c) the agent judges that, all things considered, it would be better to do y than to do x (*EAE*, p. 22; cf. p. 40).

For Davidson, the problem of incontinence is this: although there seem to be incontinent actions in this sense, their existence apparently conflicts with two self-evident principles (*EAE*, pp. 22–23). The first principle, P1, relates wanting or desiring to act to action:

P1.   If an agent wants to do x more than he wants to do y and he believes himself free to do either x or y, then he will intentionally do x if he does either x or y intentionally.

The second principle, P2, connects judgements about what it is better to do with wanting:

P2.   If an agent judges that it would be better to do x than to do y, then he wants to do x more than he wants to do y.

The logical situation then is as follows. "P1 and P2 together obviously entail that if an agent judges that it would be better for him to do x than to do y, and he believes himself to be free to do either x or y, then he will intentionally do x if he does either x or y intentionally"; and this result apparently is incompatible with the plausible claim

P3.   There are incontinent actions

where incontinence is understood as at D (*EAE*, p. 23).

Appearances, however, can be deceptive; and Davidson's strategy for solving the problem of incontinence, as he poses it, is to argue that P1–P3 do not actually form an inconsistent triad. His solution, in essence, is this: whereas P3 concerns *prima facie* (*pf*) or conditional evaluation about action, P2 concerns evaluation *sans phrase*, or unconditional evaluation, about action. It is a mistaken conception of practical reasoning, contends Davidson, which explains our inclination to confuse these two kinds of evaluation and to judge P1–P3 inconsistent (*EAE*, pp. 23–24).

We conceive of the reasoning behind all-things-considered evaluations about action as deductive reasoning in terms of universally quantified conditionals from which we can detach conclusions about what is desirable or better or some such; that is where we go wrong. The central reason that such reasoning cannot be deductive is that so construing it allows us, *per impossibile*, to derive contradictory conclusions from premises all of which are "true (or acceptable)". In fact, claims Davidson, such reasoning is reasoning in terms of conditional or relational evaluations in which prima facie functions as an operator on pairs of sentences related as (expressing) evaluation and ground. So the judgement that the akrates characteristically violates is properly construed as, "All the available relevant considerations *e* prima facie make it better to do *y* than to do *x*"; in symbols, *pf* (*y* is better than *x*, *e*). Inasmuch as practical reasoning is reasoning in terms of *pf* evaluations, Davidson's idea is, it models itself on inductive reasoning from probabilistic evidence, where a judgement like "If the barometer falls, it almost certainly will rain" is properly rendered after the fashion "That the barometer falls probabilizes that it will rain"; in symbols *pr* (*Rx, Fx*), where *x* ranges over areas of spacetime that may be characterized by falling barometers or rain (cf. *EAE*, pp. 37–39).

Practical reasoning that stops at conditional or relational judgements like the akrates' all-things-considered better judgement (the evaluation with which P3 is concerned) is, according to Davidson, insulated from intentional action: "practical only in its subject, not its issue". The judgements that are properly directly associated with intentional actions are, rather, unconditional or nonrelational evaluations like "It would be better to do *x* than to do *y*", which represent a stage in reasoning beyond *pf* conclusions: witness P1 and P2. The problem of incontinence disappears, on this story, when we appreciate the contrast between conditional and unconditional evaluative judgements and its relevance to P1–P3 (*EAE*, pp. 30–39, see also "Intending", *EAE*, pp. 97–98).

For Davidson, what happens in cases of incontinence or weakness of will is that, although the agent acts contrary to his conditional better judgement, he acts in line with his unconditional better judgement. Weakness, says Davidson, is deeply irrational. It contravenes the principle of practical reasoning: "perform the action judged best on the basis of all available relevant reasons", which Davidson dubs the "principle of continence" (*EAE*, p. 41). Furthermore, although, inasmuch as he acts intentionally, he acts for a reason (*EAE*, pp. 32–33, 39), the akrates acts without a reason for not letting his all-things-considered judgement about what is better prevail (*EAE*, p. 42). Davidson concludes: in incontinence, "the attempt to read reason into behaviour is necessarily subject to a degree of frustration"; indeed, the akrates is his own mystery: "he recognizes, in his own intentional behaviour, something essentially surd" (*EAE*, p. 42).[28]

Davidson is certainly correct about the contrast between conditional, or *pf*, evaluation and unconditional evaluation, or evaluation *sans phrase*. It is one thing to judge something simply best, and quite another to judge it best relative to some fact or facts. We need, therefore, to distinguish between conditional and unconditional summary evaluation about action. All-things-considered evaluations about action are, as Davidson observes, conditional cases. So, for example, to judge that, all things considered, it would be better to do *y* than to do *x* is effectively to judge that, relative to all the available relevant considerations, it would be better to do *y* than to do *x*. The contrasting all-out or unconditional cases are where, on the basis of what are taken to be all the available relevant considerations, someone makes a judgement about what is simply best, or right, to do, or some such.[29]

The important point for present purposes is that the putative akrates, as conceived in the terms of my original question, acts against his *all-out* or *unconditional* summary evaluation about action. Davidson's putative akrates, by contrast, acts against his *conditional* summary evaluation. This detail, as we have seen, is critical to Davidson's solution of the problem of incontinence. For then it turns out that, whereas P2 is about evaluation *sans phrase*, P3 is about *pf* evaluation, which ensures that P1–P3 are consistent. From the point of view of this essay, however, what is significant is this: given his commitment to P1–P2, Davidson too is revealed as unsympathetic to the possibility of such weakness of will as is at issue here. For, as I have just stressed, the concern I have with whether weakness is possible is specifically a concern with whether certain cases of acting against one's *unconditional* better judgement, or judgement about what is right, or some such, are possible. No doubt other putative phenomena merit being thought of in terms of weakness of will[30]; but none seem more central than the range of cases I have in mind; and moreover, it is surely these which, quite naturally, have provided the standard focus of discussions of whether weakness is possible.[31]

IV

In this essay I propose to develop the idea that the most promising strategy in support of the possibility of such weakness of will as concerns me lies with a correct interpretation of all-out present-tense summary evaluative thinking about one's own action. For, presumably, if any logically necessary relation did obtain between the putative akrates' characteristic evaluation and his having a certain volition to act (which would make weakness of will *impossible*), this would reflect something about the kind of thinking that all-out present-tense summary evaluative thinking about one's own action is. That is to say, presumably the explanation of any such conceptual nexus, if it existed, would lie, at base, in some aspect of the nature of such thinking; and what I shall argue is that there is nothing in the nature of such thinking wherein to ground any logically necessary relation between its full-fledged occurrence and the presence of a corresponding volition to act. Quite the reverse, in fact: all-out present-tense summary evaluative thinking about one's own action is such as to allow any full-fledged instance's complete dissociation from any accordant volition to act.

I am concerned to defeat, in the first place, *volitionist* construals of all-out present-tense summary evaluative judgements about one's own action; that is to say, construals of such thinking which interpret it as, at least in part, in some way volitional *in itself*. Volitionism about such evaluative thinking can be compatible with the possibility of such weakness of will as concerns me; but there are significant cases where it is not thus compatible; and, in any event, the position I take to be correct is the strong one that volitional thinking is not in any way intrinsic to all-out present-tense summary evaluative thinking about one's own action.

Volitionism, it seems to me, seduces us when we lose sight of the difference between *(e)valuating* and *valuing*. What we *value* is

what matters or is important to us. That is to say, it is only *valuing*
that implies the presence of volitional thinking. Whereas *(e)valuat-
ing* something is *merely* thinking it to be of some value, *valuing* it is
both thinking it to be of value *and* having it (for the reason that it
has such value) as an object of volition.

Davidson, interestingly, is a volitionist about present-tense
evaluative thinking about one's own action. On his current view,
as set forth in the later piece "Intending", such evaluative thinking is exhaustively divided up among the relevant practical pro
attitudes. Thus, a subclass of all-out or unconditional present-
tense evaluative judgements about one's own action are intentions to act; a subclass of prima facie or conditional present-tense
evaluations about one's own action are wants or desires to act (in a
narrow sense of "want" and "desire"), and so on.[32] Davidson's
defense of his volitionism is, however, slight. In "Intending", the
burden of this defense seems carried by the intuition that
evaluative sentences are apt for expressing practical pro attitudes[33]; and, to recommend this intuition, Davidson appeals to
the idea that having appropriate pro attitudes is a sincerity condition on evaluative illocutions. He writes:

> There is no short proof that evaluative sentences express
> desires and other pro attitudes in the way that the sentence
> 'Snow is white' expresses the belief that snow is white. But
> the following consideration will perhaps help show what is
> involved. If someone who knows English says honestly
> 'Snow is white', then he believes snow is white. If my thesis
> is correct, someone who says honestly 'It is desirable that I
> stop smoking' has some pro attitude towards his stopping
> smoking. He feels some inclination to do it; in fact he will do
> it if nothing stands in the way, he knows how, and he has
> no contrary values or desires. Given this assumption, it is
> reasonable to generalize: if explicit value judgements repre-
> sent pro attitudes, all pro attitudes may be expressed by
> value judgements that are at least implicit (*EAE*, p. 86).

The consideration invoked by Davidson in this passage is
hardly impressive. For it is questionable that paradox attaches to

saying something like "It's desirable that I stop smoking, but so what?" in the way it evidently does to saying such things as "Snow is white, but I don't think it is", "Leave the room at once, but I don't want you to", "I'll do it, but I don't have any intention to", and so on, where one apparently proceeds to deny the presence of the mental attitude whose presence is the sincerity condition on the illocution one has just performed. There is, to be sure, a clear sense in which having an attitude of approval, or pro attitude, toward stopping smoking *is* a sincerity condition on someone's saying "It's desirable that I stop smoking", namely, having the relevant positive evaluative *belief* is a sincerity condition on such an evaluative illocution. Hence it is unquestionably paradoxical to say something like "It's desirable that I stop smoking, but I don't think it is". But it is far from clear that, similarly, having a pro attitude, as a practical, that is, inherently motivational, attitude, is a sincerity condition on such an evaluative illocution.

Hare too appeals to evaluative language for support for his volitionism about all-out present-tense summary evaluative thinking about one's own action. For Hare there is a general story here. Evaluative sentences apt for expressing all-out present-tense summary evaluative thinking about action, one's own and others', semantically incorporate both indicative and imperative moods; and insofar as this is so, the corresponding evaluative thinking is revealed as, in part, cognitive or theoretical, and, in part, volitional.

In Chapter 2, I argue that evaluative language cannot be credited in this way with marking the (partial) volitional identity of all-out present-tense summary evaluative thinking about action; for the relevant evaluative sentences, demonstrably, do not quite generally have an imperative or prescriptive *volitive-mood* element in their meaning. Fundamentally, such evaluative illocutions as we characteristically perform directly[34] in uttering *bona fide* examples of such evaluatives can be entirely dissociated from *directive* illocutionary force.[35] In Chapter 3, I argue that the evaluatives corresponding to all-out present-tense summary evaluative thinking about action, one's own and others', are, one and all, *exclusively indicatives*. It is undeniable that such evaluatives *are* indicatives. For no relevant direct evaluative illocution can be dissociated from *representative* illocutionary force:[36] no speaker can say, coherently, "I (you, etc) ought to do *x*, but I'm not saying that this is so". To his credit, Hare sees this. But what emerges, I contend, is that indicatives, which are appropriate expressions in language for cognitive or theoretical thinking, that is, *beliefs*, are *all* that the evaluatives in question ever are; that they never, in addition, incorporate any relevant volitive mood; and so all-out present-tense summary evaluative thinking about action, one's own and others', is revealed, in the language of its expression, as *purely cognitive* or *theoretical* thinking.

There is a preliminary task here, however. Hare's volitionism is insensitive to certain differences within volitive language about future action, that is, the language apt for expressing volitional thinking about future action. These differences require sorting out. Briefly, for Hare, first-person singular imperative meaning marks a certain volition to act as an ingredient in full-fledged all-out present-tense summary evaluative thinking about one's own action. But it seems a mistake to think that what we are thinking when we have a volition to act is expressible as an imperative. Imperatives, rather, are appropriate volitives for expressing only intentions and desires about the future action of *others*. Self-directed volitions about future action, by contrast, are appropriately expressed in words by *intentive* and *conative* volitives like, respectively, "I will (shall) do *x*" and, perhaps, "I would do *x*". Such subjunctives of the will about future action as imperatives, intentives, and conatives contrast with *optative* volitives, which are sentences suitable for putting into words so-called "idle wishes" about *faits accomplis*.[37]

In Chapter 3, I argue that, with these differences within volitive language respected, the following becomes clear: neither the evaluatives apt for expressing all-out present-tense summary evaluative thinking about one's own action nor those apt for expressing such thinking about someone else's action incorporate either the imperative or the intentive or conative moods of the will. In sum: in both the self- and the other-directed case, such evaluative illocutions as we characteristically directly perform in uttering *bona fide* examples of the relevant evaluatives can be entirely detached from directive, and both commissive and conative,[38] illocutionary force. In consequence, the corresponding all-out present-tense summary evaluative thinking about action is revealed, in both the self- and the other-referring case, as wholly nonvolitional, that is, as involving neither self- nor other-directed volitions about future action. The relevant evaluatives are *only* what they undeniably are, namely, indicatives; and correlatively, the evaluative thinking such evaluatives are apt for expressing is *only* what it undeniably is, namely, cognitive or theoretical thinking.

This is an important result for the possibility of such weakness of will as concerns me.[39] For, characteristically, we have seen, there are two chief souces of concern about this possibility: the idea that there is an analytic connection between the putative akrates' full-fledged all-out summary evaluative thinking about action and certain volitional thinking on his part, and the further idea that there is an analytic connection between such volitional thinking and intentional action. The latter supposed connection and its cognates are themselves notoriously problematic. For they, typically, would connect volitions to act with intentional action, or attempts at such, given certain conditions; and it is questionable how, if at all, to specify these conditions, and what the status of the relevant conditionals is.[40] However, the previous result— namely, that, like such thinking about another's action, all-out present-tense summary evaluative thinking about one's own action is wholly theoretical and nonvolitional—significantly dislodges the initial source of worry about the possibility of weakness. For we can be assured, in this case, that full-fledged all-out present-tense summary evaluative thinking about his own action, such as characterizes the putative akrates, is never prevented from coming apart from some consonant volition to act on his part, by the way in which the inherently volitional character of all-out present-tense summary evaluative thinking about one's own action guarantees a logically necessary *because essential* relation between any full-fledged instance and having such a matching volition to act.

V

Perhaps this much will be conceded, but it may be contended that, even so, there is a logically necessary, albeit *extrinsic*, connection between the putative akrates' characteristic evaluation and the presence of some corresponding volition to act, at least where such evaluation is *justificatorily felicitous* all-out summary evaluation. By "justificatorily felicitous" (hereafter, felicitous) all-out summary evaluation I mean all-out summary evaluation that is ultimately grounded in some consideration, or set of considerations, that *can* serve ultimately to justify such thinking. This suggestion is reminiscent of writers like Plato and Aristotle; perhaps John Stuart Mill believed something like it.[41] What seems to be centrally at issue is, first, whether full-fledged felicitous all-out present-tense summary evaluative thinking about one's own action necessarily corresponds to, in Kantian terms, certain assertorial hypothetical imperative (ahi) thinking; and second, whether, if this is the case, such ahi thinking necessarily motivates one, in combination with the relevant antecedent volition, to form some consonant volition to act. By *ahi thinking*, I mean utilitarian judgements wherein the existence of present value in one's acting a certain way, or present reason for one so to act, is relativised to the satisfaction or achievement of certain anterior volitions or ends (objects of volition) that one actually has. Such judgements, it will be clear, are, on my view, *indicatively* expressible; but it is convenient and historically apt to refer to them in brief as *ahi judgements*.

A preliminary comment here is that it is problematic whether there is any such thing as logical necessitation of the will to subsidiary volition by means of anterior volition and relevant utilitarian evaluation.[42] The question, it seems, becomes especially acute for certain cases involving prior *intention*.[43] Classically, such a thesis of logical necessitation is associated with Kant; yet Kant, it is noteworthy, appears at times to allow for a breakdown in the transmission of will from ends to (believed) necessary means, and hence to opt for only qualified logical necessitation. For example, in the *Fundamental Principles of the Metaphysic of Morals* (FP) Kant declares:

> Whoever wills the end wills also (*so far as reason decides his conduct*) the means in his power which are indispensably necessary thereto. This proposition is, as regards the volition, analytical (p. 34; my italics).

But subsequently he characterizes his position in this way:

> . . . but if I know that it is only by this process that the intended operation can be performed, then to say that if I fully will the operation, I also will the action required first, is an analytical proposition; for it is one and the same thing to conceive something as an effect which I can produce in a certain way, and to conceive myself as acting in this way (p. 35).[44]

Among contemporary philosophers Georg Henrik von Wright is notably one for whom the question of logical necessitation has been a principal preoccupation:[45] from an original position of sympathy,[46] von Wright has come to reject its existence.[47]

Fortunately, this issue is not one we need to resolve here. For what in any case decisively undercuts the kind of proposal presently under consideration is that it cannot be sustained that full-fledged all-out present-tense summary evaluation about one's own action, even where felicitous, necessarily corresponds to ahi thinking. Quite simply: all-out present-tense summary evaluative thinking about one's own action can be felicitous and yet fail to be ultimately grounded in ahi thinking. That this is so can be seen in the following way. All-out present-tense summary evaluation about one's own action is analysable in terms of all-out summary judgements about present reason for oneself to act. I argue for this in Chapter 4. The evaluatives apt for expressing such thinking are indicatives that incorporate primary or base evaluative terms like *good, right, ought,* and the like; and such evaluative terms, as applied to actions, are analysable in terms of the concept of reason.

So, for example, to ascribe *goodness* to a future action on one's part is to say that there is *much reason for* one's performing it; to say that it is (*all*) *right* for one to do something is to say there is *sufficient reason for* one's doing it; and to say of an action that one *ought* to perform it is to say that it is what there is *most reason for* one to do. To summarize the argument here briefly, *good* means *of great,* or *high, value; right* means *of sufficient value;* and *ought* means *of most value.* The semantic common denominator here is *of value.* *x*'s being of value is tantamount to *x*'s being such that there is *something to be said for x;* and this is *x*'s being such that there is *some reason for x,* where *x* is something upon which reasons coherently can be said to bear. Persons' actions, including one's own, are paradigm examples of things for which there can be reasons for and against.

These considerations establish that all-out present-tense summary evaluations about one's own action are, in effect, all-out summary judgements about present reason for oneself to act. There is, however, no universal logical or conceptual constraint on felicitous cases of such judgements, requiring that they be ultimately grounded in ahi judgements. That is the heart of the matter. I argue the case for this in Chapter 5. Morality may well provide one way to see this truth. It is a contentious issue whether felicitous judgements about present moral reason for oneself to act are necessarily ahi judgements. For my part, I think there is reason to doubt this; and such judgements about moral reasons would seem perfectly able to serve as ultimate justifications for all-out summary judgements about present reason for oneself to act. In any event, to make the present point, we need only appeal to judgements about present prudential or self-interested reason for oneself to act. For it is surely the case that all-out summary judgements about present reason for oneself to act perfectly well admit such prudential judgements as their ultimate justifying grounds; and yet it is logically or conceptually open for one *not* to have any present concern for or interest in (promoting) one's own interest or good. One can be indifferent or hostile toward (the promotion of) one's own interest or good, just as one can be indifferent or hostile toward (the promotion of) the interest or good of another.[48]

To sum up: a correct interpretation of all-out present-tense summary evaluative thinking about one's own action undermines any suggestion that there is, universally, a logically necessary *extrinsic* relation between its full-fledged felicitous occurrence and the presence of some corresponding volition to act. For such a suggestion would seem fundamentally to rely on the idea that the evaluation in question necessarily corresponds to certain ahi thinking. But this is demonstrably false. For all-out present-tense summary evaluative thinking about one's own action perfectly well can be felicitous and yet not ultimately grounded in ahi judgements. This shows up in the relation between such evaluative thinking and corresponding judgements about present reason for oneself to act. Such evaluative thinking is analysable in terms of such judgements, and felicitous all-out summary judgements about present reason for oneself to act need not ultimately be grounded in ahi judgements. Witness, most decisively, the prudential case. Of course, it may be that there is *sometimes* a problem about the possibility of weakness of will where an agent's all-out present-tense summary evaluation about his own action does indeed correspond to an ahi evaluation on his part; but then that would be, so to speak, a *local* logical problem, relating, in its origin, in large part, to the nature of the antecedent volition that *happens* to be involved—for example, to the nature of an intention to act as a total commitment of the will to future action.[49]

VI

The solution to the problem about whether such weakness of will as is under discussion is ever possible rests with these generic facts about all-out present-tense summary evaluative thinking about one's own action: such evaluation is wholly theoretical and nonvolitional, and, without infelicity, can fail to be ultimately grounded in ahi thinking. The force of these facts, so far as concerns the possibility of weakness, is that they defeat any suggestion that the putative akrates' characteristic evaluation is analytically connected with corresponding volitional thinking.

I offer the second part of this solution from within the interpretative context of, broadly, an Aristotelian-Humean commitment about motivation by theoretical thinking, or belief, namely, that such motivation consists, fully, in motivation by belief (and ultimately ahi judgement) in combination with anterior volition to which it is suitably related.[50] The underlying view here is that, for belief, which represents a commitment about what *is the case*, to constitute a motivational influence, and hence an effective motive, it is necessary for it to connect up appropriately with some prior commitment, more or less strong, about what *to do*. For only then, the idea is, is the mental stage set for a belief to figure in practical reasoning in such a way as to help produce at least a tendency to act in a certain way, or form a corresponding volition. The picture here, of course, is that where belief does so operate as a motive it *combines coopoeratively* in practical reasoning with the prior volition to which it is suitably related. Now the view that belief alone is motivationally inert is not without its challengers; in particular, it has been opposed with specific reference to the operation of all-out present-tense summary evaluative thinking about one's own action as a *self-sufficient motive*. It therefore becomes fitting to say something about this before proceeding to the detail of my argument in the chapters to follow.

Challengers to the view that belief is motivationally impotent without antecedent volition typically fail to address themselves to the puzzle of *how* belief alone can make a motivational difference to someone; insofar as this is so, their arguments are characteristically unpersuasive.[51] Kant's position becomes interesting here. For Kant offers a binary account of rational motivation. Kant has no quarrel with the idea that it is a condition on judgement as the issue of *theoretical*, or *empirical practical*, reason if it is to have motivational influence, that it possess a suitable connection with already existing volition. His position is that there occurs also judgement as the issue of *pure practical* reason, and that this *sui generis* categorical imperative "judgement" can by itself influence the will and action.

Theoretical reason, for Kant, is reason conceived as that faculty which, in its judgements, is concerned with determining what is the case. Practical reason, in his terms, is reason conceived as that faculty which, in its judgements, can influence the will and action. Kant then distinguishes between empirical practical and pure practical reason. Insofar as empirical practical reason has motivational influence, his position is, this derives from its connection, through its judgements, with already existing interests. These judgements assume, in hypothetical imperative form, the characteristic linguistic garb of judgements of practical reason, but they are, or virtually are, theoretical.[52] By contrast, pure practical reason, in Kant's view, is an independent causal power with respect to the will and action (*FP*, pp. 14, 65, 78–79).

Kant, then, does not dispute the thesis that belief, as theoretical thinking, is by itself motivationally impotent. What he effectively does is isolate out a subclass of all-out present-tense summary evaluative judgements about one's own action—so-called categorical imperatives—for special *practical* treatment as independent motives. But, of course, the critical issue is what reason there is to follow Kant in admitting the existence of such a class of motivationally *sui generis* evaluations; and, for my part, I do not see any reason to follow him at this point.

It is sometimes suggested that Kant may have compromised his thesis that pure practical reason is an independent causal power by postulating that, where there is motivation by pure practical reason, there is subjective determination of the will by pure respect for the law, which is an interest or feeling—indeed, as Kant conceives matters, an hedonistic interest or feeling (*FP*, pp. 18, 77–78).[53] But it is implausible to claim that Kant self-contradictorily concedes what he explicitly denies for motivation by pure practical reason despite the presence of such desire, namely, "heteronomy and dependence of practical reason on sensibility" (*FP*, p. 78). It seems, rather, that Kant thereby merely postulates something in accord with his general commitment as regards *phenomenal* motivation, that is, at source, heteronomous motivation by hedonistic desire. Kant would distinguish between the will and action as belonging to the intellectual world—the will and action as noumena—and the will and action as belonging to the sensible world—the will and action as phenomena (*FP*, pp. 67 ff); and his thesis about pure practical reason being, in its judgements, an independent causal power with respect to the will and action is meant to apply to the *noumenal* will and *noumenal* action. In cases of motivation by pure practical reason, the idea is, an exercise of pure practical reason by itself moves the noumenal will, and pure respect for the law, the subjective effect of this exercise of pure reason, moves the phenomenal will (*FP*, pp. 18–19, 77 ff).[54]

No. The problem with Kant is not a problem of internal consistency. The noumenal/phenomenal partition takes care of that. The real problem is the way in which Kant's thesis that pure practical reason is an independent causal power is tied to his consistency preserving noumenal/phenomenal bifurcation of the will, action, and causation, and meant to apply at the noumenal level. For the suggestion that there is a distinct class of evaluative judgements capable by themselves of motivating to corresponding desire or action is, in any case, a dark one; and on Kant's noumenal restriction, it becomes *in principle* inilluminable, just as it becomes *in principle* inilluminable how pure practical reason can, in its exercises, have phenomenal volitional effects (*FP*, pp. 78–80).

Thomas Nagel is a contemporary philosopher who opposes the thesis that belief alone cannot be a motive in his intriguing book, *The Possibility of Altruism* (*PA*). Nagel is of special interest from the standpoint of this essay for his challenge to the view in question effectively relies on a *universal* construal of all-out present-tense summary evaluative thinking about one's own action, such as characterizes the putative akrates, as a *self-sufficient motive*. In Nagel's story, judgements about present reason for oneself to act, which he accepts as evaluations about action, bear the brunt of motivation. Reminiscent of Kant on categorical imperatives, Nagel develops an idiosyncratic *internalism* (ch. 2, pp. 7 ff),[55] according to which such judgements about reason for acting are interpreted as practical, that is, inherently motivational, even though not themselves intrinsically volitional. For Nagel, what is crucial for a belief to become constituted as a self-sufficient motive with respect to volition, or corresponding action, is that it interact, independently of already present desire, with one's system of prima facie reasons for action to (help) yield a judgement about present prima facie reason for oneself to act. Such judgements, in turn, are capable of supporting all-out judgements about present sufficient reason for oneself to act (all-out present-tense summary evaluations about one's own action), which are self-sufficient motives (*PA*, ch. 3, p. 14; ch. 5, pp. 31–32; ch. 6, p. 35; ch. 7, pp. 49–50; ch. 8, pp. 64–67).

It is noteworthy that Nagel, unlike Kant, proposes a unitary account of motivation. There is, so to speak, pure and mixed motivation *by reason*. *Pure* rational motivation is motivation by belief without any prior motivating factor by means of an all-out judgement about present sufficient reason for oneself to act. *Mixed* rational motivation is motivation by desire plus connected belief by means of an all-out judgement about present sufficient reason for oneself to act. Such judgements about such reason for acting are self-sufficient motives, that is, factors capable by themselves of motivating to intentional action or to corresponding desire. In pure rational motivation they do so motivate regardless of prior desire, and the basis of the motivation is simply belief. In mixed rational motivation, by contrast, they motivate together with desire, and the source of the motivation is desire, which, in such a case, provides a datum for practical reasoning. In *all* such motivation by reason the pivotal dynamic is the interaction of factors such as volitions and beliefs with one's system of reasons for action to (help) yield judgements about present reason for oneself to act (*PA*, ch. 5, pp. 31–32; ch. 6, pp. 33–35; ch. 8, pp. 64–67; ch. 9, p. 81; ch. 11, pp. 109–11).[56] In *The Possibility of Altruism*, Nagel argues that the characteristic possibility of pure prudence and pure altruism, that is, of our being motivated to appropriate desire or action simply by beliefs about the future consequences (*PA*, ch. 6, pp. 36–37) or consequences for others, of our actions, is something that can be explained in terms of how the presence in us of the system of prima facie reasons for action on which these possibilities depend relates to basic features of our makeup as humans.[57]

There is much in the fine-grained detail of Nagel's defense of the possibility of pure prudence and pure altruism that is debatable.[58] My focus, however, is on Nagel's internalist construal of all-out judgements about present sufficient reason for oneself to act as practical, or inherently motivational, inasmuch as these judgements are capable by themselves of motivating to desire or action. For it is, at base, with reference to this interpretation of such judgements that Nagel would explain the presence of beliefs as volitionally independent motives; yet it seems to me that he does not make good this crucial practical identification of such judgements.

Nagel's line of argument in this connection is not especially perspicuous; but I think the following is a fair reconstruction. The heart of the matter is whether all-out judgements about present sufficient reason for oneself to act are to count as conclusions of genuine practical reasoning, that is, as practical judgements about what *to do*. It is given that the motivational content of practical judgements about what to do consists in their being by themselves sufficient to explain accordant desire or action, in the absence of contrary influences; in other words, in their being, in the absence of contrary influences, capable by themselves of motivating to such desire or action. Such practical judgements about what to do are self-sufficient motives in this way, according to Nagel, inasmuch as they constitute *the acceptance of a justification* for doing or wanting something. It seems most plausible, he thinks, to suppose that all-out judgements about present sufficient reason for oneself to act are, in addition to theoretical classificatory judgements (cf. Hare), just such practical judgements about what to do (cf. Kant) (*PA*, ch. 8, pp. 64–67; ch. 11, pp. 109–11; ch. 12, p. 121).

To my mind it is counterintuitive to admit, as Nagel wishes to admit, a distinction between judgements about present sufficient reason for acting and judgements about present justification for acting, so that the latter are merely elements in the former. But let that be. Nagel is impressed by the idea that all-out judgements about present sufficient reason for oneself to act are inherently relevant to decisions about what to do (*PA*, pp. 109–10). This can be acknowledged, it is worth remarking, without endorsing *any* version of internalism. For, quite simply, such judgements present themselves as judgements about the merit of, or reason attaching to, possible actions by us, and hence, corresponding possible decisions on our part. But what is finally unsatisfactory here is reminiscent of what is finally unsatisfactory about Kant's position. For Nagel proposes that there is a distinct category of practical judgements—with which he identifies all-out judgements about present sufficient reason for oneself to act—which, in rational motivation, mediate between beliefs and other types of motives, on the one hand, and resultant desires to act or actions, on the other; that is to say, which are capable by themselves of motivating to desire or action, in the absence of countervailing factors; and the question is what to make of this curious proposal.

Nagel, for his part, relies heavily on the idea that such practical judgements are conclusions or judgements about what *to do*. But this hardly helps. For conclusions or "judgements" about what to do are naturally interpreted in terms of such *volitions* as correspond to directive and commissive illocutions, those illocutions which characteristically constitute direct answers in speech to questions of what to do, one's own and others'. Indeed, the idea that all-out judgements about present sufficient reason for oneself to act, or all-out present-tense summary evaluations about one's own action, are, or involve, conclusions or judgements about what to do naturally belongs to the defense of *volitionist* internalism. Hare is right on this score.

To conclude: the position which I take to be correct and which is assumed by the second part of the solution I offer to the problem of whether weakness of will is ever possible, is that the existence of an appropriate connection (ultimately via ahi thinking) with antecedent volition, or practical thinking, is critical to the functioning of theoretical thinking, or belief, as a motive. It is a puzzle how belief, which represents merely a commitment about what *is the case* and not about what *to do*, can make a motivational difference to someone without some such relation to prior volition; and neo-Kantian suggestions like Nagel's—that it is possible for belief to function motivationally, as independent support for partially practical all-out judgements about present sufficient reason for oneself to act—are unpersuasive.

CHAPTER TWO

Evaluatives, Imperatives
and Evaluative Thinking

THE CENTRAL THEME of this chapter and the next is that evaluative
sentences like "I (you, he, etc.) ought to do x", "The right thing
for me (you, him, etc.) to do is to do x", and so on, do not contain a
volitive-mood element in their meaning but are exclusively indicative, and that, therefore, the evaluative judgements they are
apt for expressing, namely, all-out present-tense summary
evaluative judgements about action, are *purely* cognitive or
theoretical. The lesson here, so far as concerns the possibility of
weakness of will, is the anti-volitionist one that there is no logically necessary *because constitutive* relation between such
evaluative thinking as characterizes the putative akrates and the
presence in him of a corresponding volition to act. R. M. Hare
contends that evaluative sentences apt for expressing all-out
present-tense summary evaluation about action, one's own and
others', semantically incorporate the indicative and imperative
moods, and that, inasmuch as this is so, the correlative evaluative
thinking is revealed as partially cognitive and partially volitional.
In the present chapter, I wish to argue in particular that such
evaluatives do not contain an imperative-mood element in their
meaning and, hence, do not in this way indicate the partially volitional character of all-out present-tense summary evaluation
about action.

I

Hare's thesis that evaluatives like "I (you, he, etc.) ought to
do x" contain an imperative semantic component is itself an

aspect of a quite general story about the meaning and semantic contribution to sentences of evaluative words. This general *prescriptivist* story receives its classic articulation by Hare in his two books, *The Language of Morals* (*LM*, 1952) and *Freedom and Reason* (*FR*, 1963). Evaluative words, we are told in these two works, have both descriptive and prescriptive meaning (*LM* 5 ff; *FR* 2). Some evaluative words are such that their descriptive meaning is primary, for example, *industrious* and *courageous* (*LM* 7.5, pp. 121 ff; *FR* 2.7, p. 24). Others are such that, characteristically, their prescriptive meaning is primary, for example, *good, right,* and *ought* (*LM* 7.4 pp. 118 ff; 10.4, p. 158 ff; *FR* 2.7, pp. 23–25). When we evaluate something, says Hare, we necessarily do so because of certain properties it has. Such "virtues" (in the positive case) make up the ground of our evaluation, and the descriptive meaning of an evaluative term, when we apply it to something, is determined by such "virtues" as we reckon that thing to possess. So, for example, the descriptive meaning of *good* in a sentence like "This is a good strawberry" might be *sweet, juicy, firm, red, and large* (*LM* 5–10, *passim*; *FR* 2, pp. 15 ff).[1] It is in virtue of the descriptive meaning of the evaluative terms they contain, according to Hare, that evaluative judgements are universalizable (*FR* 2, pp. 10 ff). In addition to such descriptive meaning, says Hare, evaluative terms have prescriptive meaning. So, for example, knowing the meaning of *good* in a categorical affirmative like "This is a good *x*" includes knowing that to call *x* good is to *commend* it, that the incorporation of *good* into a sentence like that invests it with the property that its (literal) utterance would be a commendation of *x* (a species of prescription, or guide to choice or conduct). What this comes to in effect is that it is an aspect of the meaning of an evaluative term like *good* that it introduces the *imperative mood* in a particular way into a categorical affirmative like "This is a good *x*" (*LM* 5 ff, esp. 7 ff; *FR* 2). Similarly for an evaluative word like *ought*. Knowing the meaning of *ought* involves knowing that its incorporation into a sentence like "I ought to do *x*" gives to that sentence the property that its (literal) utterance would be a (possibly downgraded) prescription, or guide to choice or conduct; one would know that its inclusion in such a categorical affirmative embeds the imperative mood within it at some level of prescriptivity (*LM* 10–11; *FR* 2.5).

In Hare's 1970 paper "Meaning and Speech Acts" (MSA),[2] prescriptivism occurs as part of a wider story about speech-act analyses of the meanings of certain words. Prescriptivism, of course, represents the story with respect to evaluative words. Hare characterizes speech-act analyses this way:

> The performers put forward theories of the following general type: they claim that the meaning of a certain word can be explained, or partly explained, by saying that, when incorporated in an appropriate sentence in an appropriate place, it gives to that whole sentence the property that an utterance of it would be, in the appropriate context, a performance of a certain kind of speech act. This is the same as to say that the utterance would have, in Austin's term, a certain illocutionary force; and it is the same as to say, with Professor Alston, that the sentence has a certain illocutionary-act potential. Thus, to take Searle's relatively uncontroversial example, the incorporation of the word 'promise' in that particular place in the sentence (that particular sentence) 'I promise to pay you $5 tomorrow' gives to that whole sentence the property that an utterance of it would be, in an appropriate context, a performance of the speech act of promising to pay the person addressed $5 on the day following the utterance; and, it is claimed, to say this is to say something (not necessarily everything) about the meaning of the word 'promise' (MSA, p. 75).

According to Hare, the elucidation of part of the meaning of an evaluative term like *good* follows suit. In the case of *good*, the relevant speech-act is the species of prescription, commendation (MSA, pp. 75–76).

II

The task now is to assess prescriptivism. What becomes clear is that this theory of evaluative meaning is a worthy opponent. Prescriptivism effectively identifies the prescriptive meaning of evaluative words like *good*, *ought*, and *right* with imperative-mood meaning. Now the speech-act analysis of mood meaning has itself been challenged—for example, by David Holdcroft in *Words and Deeds*.[3] This is somewhat surprising given what seems to be the "primary, essential function" of mood signs as indicators of standard illocutionary force.[4] Holdcroft, curiously, thinks that, whereas the meaning of performative prefixes can be explained by reference to illocutionary force, mood meaning cannot.[5] For Holdcroft, for example, the meaning conveyed by the indicative-mood indicator is that the sentence containing it has truth conditions (ch. 4, pp. 57–58), whereas the meaning conveyed by the imperative-mood sign is that the sentence to which it is attached has conformity conditions (ch. 6, pp. 97 ff, esp. 100). The point is reminiscent of Anthony Kenny's division in *Action, Emotion and Will*, between indicatives and optatives in terms of the differences in direction of fit between words and the world.[6]

Holdcroft's position, however, its unconvincing.[7] For, although it can be agreed that, for example, indicatives are semantically associated with truth conditions, this seems a *derivative* fact about such sentences which can be explained by an analysis of indicative meaning in terms of illocutionary-force potential. For indicatives, so understood, are those sentences which, in virtue of containing an indicative main verb, have it as part of their meaning that their literal utterances standardly constitute saying that something is the case, that is, representing or describing things as being a certain way. Accordingly, it becomes semantically given as an issue, distinctively, for indicatives, as used literally to say something, whether they are being used to represent or describe things the way they are—that is, whether they are being used to say something true. Similarly for imperatives and their semantic association with conformity conditions. For again, this seems to be a derivative fact about imperatives which can be explained by an analysis of imperative meaning in terms of illocutionary-force potential. Imperatives, so interpreted, are those sentences which, in virtue of containing an imperative main verb, have it as part of their meaning that their literal utterances typically are cases of saying to someone that he do something. Accordingly, it becomes an issue for imperatives, as used literally to say something, whether they—or better, the prescriptives or directives they express—are conformed to or complied with (obeyed, heeded, followed, etc.) by their addressees in what they subsequently do.

Holdcroft, in fact, is committed to a certain modification of his original bare claim that the meaning of the imperative-mood sign is that the sentence to which it is attached has conformity conditions. For he also wants to say that sentences like ''I will/shall be there'' sometimes incorporate a commissive (which I prefer to call *intentive*[8]) mood indicator whose meaning can be given in terms of such sentences' possessing conformity conditions (ch. 7, pp. 119–21). Holdcroft's thesis becomes, more strictly, it seems, that imperative meaning is specifiable in terms of *addressee* conformity conditions, whereas commissive meaning is specifiable in terms of *speaker* conformity conditions. In respect of such an account of commissive or intentive meaning there are points to be made similar to those made in the previous two cases. Commissive or intentive sentences undeniably are sematically associated with speaker conformity conditions, but this is a secondary fact about such sentences which can be explained by an analysis of commissive or intentive meaning in terms of illocutionary-force potential. For commissives or intentives, so understood, are those sentences which, in virtue of containing a principal verb in the commissive or intentive mood, have it as part of their meaning that their literal utterances standardly are cases of committing oneself to doing something. Accordingly, it is semantically given as a question for commissives or intentives, as used literally to say something, whether they—or better, the self-commitments to future action they express—are conformed to or complied with (kept to, carried out, honoured, respected, heeded, etc.) by their speakers in what they subsequently do.

To sum up so far: prescriptivism is tied to the speech-act analysis of mood meaning. This seems a very plausible approach to understanding the meaning that attaches to the verbal syntactic forms associated with mood in the light of the fundamental role of such mood signs as indicators of standard illocutionary force; and a counterthesis like Holdcroft's does not successfully impugn it. If there is a legitimate argument against prescriptivism in this connection, I would say, it has, rather, to do with the idea, which surfaces in the prescriptivist account of *good*, that mood meaning is sometimes specifiable in terms of specific or particular illocutionary-force potential, for example, commendatory illocutionary-force potential; whereas what seems correct is that mood meaning connects with *generic* illocutionary-force potential.[9]

A serious charge against the speech-act analysis of *good* is that it cannot meet the requirement on any such semantic account that it allow for *good* to be univocal throughout its sentential contexts of occurrence. Indeed, a chief concern of Hare's in the paper ''Meaning and Speech Acts'' is to discuss this charge. It is clear that the requirement holds. Otherwise, for example, ''This is not a good *x*'' would not count as the denial of ''This is a good *x*'', ''This is a good *x*'' would not count as an answer to ''Is this a good *x*?'', and the *modus ponens* inference from the conjunction of ''If this is a good *x*, then *p* is the case'' and ''This is a good *x*'' to the conclusion ''*p* is the case'' would suffer from a fallacy of equivocation (MSA, pp. 76–77).

John Searle is a notable example of someone who has laid the charge in question against the speech-act analysis of *good*, and certain other words, in contrast to the speech-act analysis of explicit performative verbs like *commend, promise*, etc.[10] Searle writes, in *Speech Acts* (*SA*, 1970):

> Now, there is a condition of adequacy which any analysis of the meaning of a word must meet—and which the speech act analysis fails to meet. Any analysis of the meaning of a word (or morpheme) must be consistent with the fact that the same word (or morpheme) can mean the same thing in all the grammatically different kinds of sentences in which it can occur. Syntactical transformations of sentences do not necessarily enforce changes of meaning on the component words or morphemes of those sentences (6.2, p. 187).

Searle's worry is not that, for example, literal utterances of *good* are not always associated with acts of commendation. He develops his criticism in these terms:

More precisely, to satisfy the condition of adequacy, the speech act analysts do not need to show that every utterance of *W* is a performance of *A*, but rather they need only to show that literal utterances which are not performances of the act *A* stand in a relation to performances of *A* in a way which is purely a function of the way the sentences uttered stand in relation to the standard indicative sentences, in the utterance of which the act is performed. If they are in the past tense, then the act is reported in the past; if they are hypothetical, then the act is hypothesized, etc. (*SA* 6.2, p. 138).

What Searle contends is that, whereas the speech-act analysis of performative verbs satisfies this condition in this way, the analogous analyses of *good*, etc., do not. He writes:

For example, when one says something of the form, "If he promises that *p*, then so and so", he hypothesizes the performance of the act which he performs when he says something of the form, "I promise that *p*". But it is equally clear that the speech act analysis of the other words: "good", "true", "probable", etc., does not satisfy this condition. Consider the following examples: "If this is good, then we ought to buy it", is not equivalent to "If I commend this, then we ought to buy it". "This used to be good" is not equivalent to "I used to commend this". "I wonder whether this is good" is not equivalent to "I wonder whether I commend this", etc. (*SA* 6.2, pp. 138–39).

In "Meaning and Speech Acts" Hare attempts to show that, *pace* Searle and others, the speech-act analysis of *good* can meet the relevant condition of adequacy. The picture that emerges (MSA, pp. 77–89) is as follows. It is part of the meaning of *good* in a categorical affirmative like "This is a good *x*" that its incorporation into that sentence gives to the whole sentence the property that an utterance of it would be, in an appropriate context, a performance of the speech-act of commending *x*. This, according to Hare, is basic to the meaning of the negative, interrogative, and subordinate clause syntactical transformations of such a sentence. For example, explaining the meaning of a sentence like "This is not a good x", construed as the internal negation of "This is a good x", involves connecting up the commendatory meaning of *good* in the corresponding affirmative with the meaning conveyed by the particular transformation, internal negation. This yields as a partial explanation of the meaning of the negative in question that its utterance would be, in an appropriate context, a performance of the speech-act that is the internal negation of commendation. Similarly for an interrogative like "Is this a good x?". Knowing the meaning of such a sentence involves, in part, knowing the commendatory meaning of *good* in the corresponding categorical affirmative and the meaning conveyed by the particular transformation, the interrogative sentence form. For then we know that the meaning of "Is this a good x?" can be explained, in part, by saying that its utterance would be, in an appropriate context, an invitation to say either "This is a good x" (which is a commendation) or "This is not a good x" (which is the negation of a commendation). Consider, finally, a sentence like "If this is a good x, then p is the case". Knowing the meaning of such a hypothetical, on the current story, involves knowing (1) the meaning of the hypothetical sentence form and (2) the meanings of the encaged categoricals. Knowing the first, according to Hare, comes to understanding the operation of *modus ponens* and related inferences; to know the second, one must know, *inter alia*, that utterances of the categorical affirmative "This is a good x" are, in the absence of contextual countersigns, commendatory illocutions.

It seems to me that in these comments Hare has bested critics like Searle and has shown that prescriptivism is not in the least unequal to the requirement on any account of the meaning of an evaluative term like *good* that it be compatible with the word's being univocal throughout syntactical transformations of categoricals like "This is a good x". In the case of *good*, for example, prescriptivism simply maintains that, throughout such occurrences, it is part of the meaning of that word that it invests the relevant transformationally basic categorical affirmative with commendatory illocutionary-force potential. There is, indeed, something very peculiar about the way in which Searle argues that, whereas the speech-act analysis of performative verbs meets the condition of adequacy in question, the speech-act analysis of a word like *good* does not. This peculiarity is adverted to by Hare in his own paper. Briefly: Searle's argument irrelevantly focuses on syntactical transformations of categoricals wherein verbs like *commend* and *promise* occur *autobiographically*, that is, *descriptively*, and not on transformations of categoricals wherein such verbs have *performative* occurrences. What Hare contends, convincingly, is that the speech-act analysis of *good* fares well with respect to the relevant condition of adequacy, much as the speech-act analysis of genuine performative verbs fares well in this respect.

In the performative case, relevant sentences to consider are ones like:

(1)   I promise to do x (apt as positive promise)

(2)   I promise not to do x (apt as negative promise)

(3)   I do not promise to do x (apt as refusal to promise)

(4)   Do you promise to do x? (apt as a question which expects as answer a promise to do x or a refusal to promise to do x) (MSA, pp. 79–80).

Throughout (1)–(4), according to Hare, it is part of the meaning of *promise* that its incorporation into the categorical affirmative (1) gives to that whole sentence the property that its utterance would be, in an appropriate context, a case of promising to do x. Understanding the meaning of (2)–(4) involves, *inter alia*, understanding this as well as the different meanings of the different syntactical transformations of (1): internal negation for (2); external negation for (3); interrogative transformation for (4) (MSA, pp. 78 ff).

It will be noticed that explicit performative verbs, unlike *good*, cannot occur in conditional clauses. This, indeed, as Hare concedes, is an objection to any claim that a sentence like "This is a good x" means the same as "I commend this as an x" (MSA, pp. 88–89; see also 75–76 and 85–86). In "Meaning and Speech Acts" Hare offers an explanation of this asymmetry which represents an improvement for prescriptivism, so far as concerns the interpretation of mood and evaluative meaning, over the line he took in *The Language of Morals* and *Freedom and Reason*. For a shift occurs between those two books and the later paper as regards mood meaning: in the former, mood meaning is connected with *actual* illocutionary force; in the latter, it is connected with illocutionary-force *potential*. This, naturally, affects the prescriptivist account of evaluative meaning: in the former two works, prescriptive meaning, which corresponds to the meaning of the imperative mood, is specified with reference to *actual* prescription; in "Meaning and Speech Acts", by contrast, the prescriptive meaning of *good* is specified with reference to commendatory illocutionary-force *potential*. The critical distinction which makes all the difference here is the distinction between *sign of mood* and *sign of subscription*.

In *The Language of Morals* Hare attempts to isolate what is common to and what differentiates indicative and imperative sentences. What is common, he says, is their *phrastic* component, that part of any such sentence which refers to what it is about. What differentiates them, he says, is their *neustic* component, that part of any such sentence which determines its mood. For example, the indicative "You are about to shut the door" and the imperative "Shut the door" can be analysed in such a way as to have the same phrastic but different neustics: as

> Shutting the door by you in the immediate future, yes
> Shutting the door by you in the immediate future, please

respectively. Signs of mood, or neustics, says Hare, signify the use or affirmation of a sentence. The meaning conveyed by the indicative neustic (represented above by "yes") is that the (literal) utterance of the sentence containing it as the form of its main verb would be telling someone that something is the case. The meaning conveyed by the imperative-mood sign (represented above by "please") is that the (literal) utterance of the sentence containing it as the form of its main verb would be telling someone to make something the case (to do something) (*LM* 1–2; 12, pp. 188 ff; *FR*, p. 27; cf. too "Imperative Sentences").

In this early account Hare builds sign of subscription meaning into sign of mood meaning. This failure to keep these two separate taints prescriptivism as Hare presents it in *LM,* and later, in *FR*. For, as I have already indicated, the prescriptive aspect of the meaning of evaluative terms is, in these two works, correspondingly associated with actual rather than potential prescriptive illocutionary force. In this way, prescriptivism, in its original form, becomes liable to the kind of criticism made by Peter Geach, namely, that it unacceptably drives a semantic wedge between, for example, *good* as it occurs in unembedded categoricals like "This is a good *x*" (to whose literal utterances illocutionary force attaches) and *good* as it occurs in corresponding syntactically embedded categoricals, for example, *good* as it occurs in such categoricals embedded as conditional clauses (to whose literal utterances illocutionary force cannot attach).[11] In "Meaning and Speech Acts", by contrast, Hare is careful to present the speech-act analysis of the prescriptive meaning of *good* in a way that respects the difference between sign of mood (now called *tropic*) meaning, which is connected with illocutionary-force potential, and sign of subscription (now called *neustic*) meaning, which is connected with the issuance of an utterance with illocutionary force. In this way Hare protects prescriptivism against Geach's specific line of attack, and, more generally, prepares the ground for showing that, *pace* Searle, prescriptivism is compatible with the fact that, for example, *good* is univocal across the range of available syntactical transformations of a categorical affirmative like "This is a good *x*".

The revised story about neustics, tropics, and phrastics goes, briefly, like this (MSA, pp. 89 ff). Sentences such as indicatives and imperatives always have a phrastic part governed by a sign of mood, that is, tropic, part. They have, in addition, a sign of subscription, that is, neustic, element (expressed or understood) when they are used (as in the case of indicatives) to make assertions or (as in the case of imperatives) to issue prescriptions. As subordinate clauses, by contrast, including conditional clauses, such sentences possess phrastics and tropics, but not neustics. It is constancy in meaning between a minor premise and the antecedent of a conditional in respect of their *phrastic* and *tropic* constituents which is crucial if a logical operation like *modus ponens* is to go through. Sign of subscription meaning is an aspect of meaning irrelevant to logic. Explicit performative prefixes like "I hereby declare that" and "I hereby order you to" are combinations of neustics and tropics. In these considerations we have, according to Hare, the explanation of why explicit performative verbs, unlike *good*, cannot occur in conditional clauses. A categorical affirmative like "This is a good *x*" can shed its neustic component, retaining only its indicative and imperative tropics; but a sentence like "I (hereby) commend this as an *x*" has a fixed neustic constituent that precludes its conditional occurrence.

III

My quarry is prescriptivism because, according to this account of evaluative meaning, evaluative sentences apt for expressing such judgements as characterize the putative akrates, in line with evaluative sentences in general, have an imperative-mood element in their meaning, and insofar as this is the case, the relevant evaluative thinking, in line with evaluative thinking quite generally, is revealed as partially volitional. The position I take to be correct, by contrast, is that evaluatives are wholly indicative, and the corresponding thinking purely theoretical or cognitive. But so far we have seen that prescriptivism, as developed by Hare, is a resourceful quarry, at least with respect to the issue of how best to give an account of mood meaning, and to the charge that it pluralizes the meaning of evaluative terms like *good*. In the end, I want to say, the defeat of prescriptivism lies, not in its account of mood meaning, or in how it squares with the univocalness condition of adequacy,[12] but in the central contention that positive evaluative terms, *inter alia*, effectively introduce imperative-mood meaning into categorical affirmatives that contain them; that it is a fundamental aspect of the meaning of such terms, the prescriptive aspect, that they connect literal utterances of such categoricals with prescriptive, or, as I prefer to say, directive (see fn. 8, this chapter), illocutionary-force potential in exactly the way that imperative-mood signs connect literal utterances of imperatives with such illocutionary-force potential.[13]

By way of preliminary to developing this criticism, I should like to consider the prescriptivist emphasis on the fact that *good* is a word primarily used for commending. For prescriptivism is perhaps most seductive in its claim that a dimension of the meaning of the evaluative word *good*, as it occurs in a categorical affirmative like "This is a good *x*", is that it invests this incorporating sentence with the property that its literal utterance has, specifically, *commendatory* illocutionary-force potential. For it surely is right that the literal utterance of such a sentence, as a consequence of that sentence's incorporating *good*, has commendatory, or some kindred, illocutionary-force potential. The preliminary point I want to make against prescriptivism is that commendation, however, is not a directive (prescriptive) illocution; so the truth in question is small comfort to prescriptivism.

The syntax of *commend* supports the view that commendation is other than a directive illocution. Directive verbs, such as *command, order, request, advise, exhort,* and the like, characteristically occur in explicit performative sentences of the syntactic shape[14]

$$N_i V_i N_j \text{ to } V_j +$$

which have the deep structure

$$N_i V_i N_j + N_j \text{ subj } (V_j) +$$

For example, from the container and subjunctive matrix elements

I order you + you (should) leave at once

we derive the nominal compound

I order you to leave at once[15].

But explicit performative sentences like

I commend this movie
I commend Fred

abbreviate sentences like

> I commend this movie for being so well acted
> I commend Fred for his hard work

which have, by contrast, the syntactic form

$$N_i \; V_i \; N_j \; \text{Prep (Gerundive) Nom}$$

Nominal compounds like this represent the surface structure realization of elements of the form

$$N_i \; V_i \; N_j + N_i \, / \, N_j \; V_j +$$

Illocutionary verbs collected by this syntactic shape and corresponding deep structure are, besides *commend*, verbs like *praise, laud, extol, thank, congratulate, compliment, welcome, criticize, condemn, pardon, apologize,* and so on (Vendler, *RC*, ch. 2, pp. 23, 25; ch. 3, p. 35; Searle, *CIA*, pp. 12–13, 18).

These verbs with which *commend* has a common syntax denote illocutions that have an illocutionary point or purpose quite distinct from those denoted by directive verbs.[16] The characteristic illocutionary point or purpose of directive illocutions is to put it to addressees to make certain things the case (to act in certain ways): to say to them that they should make certain things the case (act in certain ways).[17] The characteristic illocutionary point or purpose of the illocutions presently in question, however—Searle's *expressives*[18]—is, as Searle says, to express the psychological attitudes the havings of which are the sincerity conditions on their performances. For example: the illocutionary point of my thanking you for your having helped me consists in my expressing my gratitude to you for your having so aided me; the illocutionary purpose of my congratulating you on winning the scholarship consists in my expressing my pleasure at your winning the award; the illocutionary point of my apologizing to you for having hit you so hard consists in my expressing my regret at having done this to you; and so on.[19] Of course, all illocutionary acts that have the presence of a psychological state for their sincerity condition count as expressions of that state. Just as apologies are expressions of regret, so, for example, statements are expressions of belief, orders are expressions of other-person desires or intentions, and promises are expressions of intentions to act. The point, however, is this. When we state, order, promise, etc., we perform illocutions that belong to certain general kinds, namely, representative, directive, commissive illocutions, and so on; and *also* we perform illocutions that belong to a certain *different* general kind, namely, expressive illocutions. But when we thank, congratulate, apologize, and so on, we count merely as performing a species of the genus of expressive illocutions.[20]

What, then, of commending? Commending, I think, should actually be grouped with expressive illocutions like praising, lauding, and extolling to form the expressive subcategory of *expressing approval,* just as the expressive illocutions of criticizing and condemning are intuitively grouped together within the expressive subcategory of *expressing disapproval.* In this case it becomes fairly plain why the incorporation of *good* into a categorical affirmative like ''This is a good *x*'' has the consequence for that sentence that its literal utterance characteristically is a commendation, or some kindred expressive illocution.[21] Because of what *good* means, to call *x* good is to issue a (highly) favourable evaluation of *x*; and it is a sincerity condition on such an evaluation that one correspondingly (highly) approve of *x*; and so to call *x* good is also in some way to express one's (high) approval of *x*, for example, to (highly) commend *x* (cf. Searle, *SA,* 6.5, pp. 150 ff). In short, the incorporation of *good* into a categorical affirmative like ''This is a good *x*'' semantically equips that sentence for use in evaluative illocutions which, in turn, count as expressions of (high) approval of *x*, for example, as (high) commendations of *x*.

Hare contends that the incorporation of *good* into a categorical like ''This is a good *x*'' invests that sentence with the property that its literal utterance standardly is a commendation of *x*, and that that it has such an effect is part, the prescriptive part, of the meaning of *good* in that sentence and its syntactical transformations. The above result challenges this contention. For, although it is true that including *good* in the sentence "This is a good *x*" connects literal utterances of that categorical with commendatory, or *some kindred,* illocutionary-force potential, commendation and its cognates, we see, are *expressive,* not directive, or in Hare's term, prescriptive, illocutions; so the truth in question can be granted without thereby conceding to the prescriptivist that the inclusion of *good* in a categorical like "This is a good *x*" connects its literal utterance, in the standard case, with directive or prescriptive illocutionary force.

I suspect that there is an elementary confusion in prescriptivism between commending and a quite different illocution, namely, *recommending.*[22] For recommending, doubtless, is a directive illocution. Compare my commending Bergman's *Autumn Sonata* in front of someone and my recommending that he go to that movie. The distinctively expressive illocutionary point of my commending Bergman's *Autumn Sonata* before someone would consist in my expressing to that person my approval of that movie. My recommending to that person that he go to Bergman's *Autumn Sonata,* on the other hand, would have for its distinctively directive illocutionary point my saying or putting it to him that he (should) go to that movie. A paradigm direct and explicit way for me to do this, that is, recommend to someone that he go to the Bergman movie, would be for me to say something like "I recommend (to you) that you go to Bergman's *Autumn Sonata*"; and a paradigm indirect way for me to make this recommendation would be for me to *commend* the movie—by saying, for example, "Bergman's *Autumn Sonata* is a good movie"—or to *express approval* of my addressee's going to it—by saying, for example, "You would do well to go to Bergman's *Autumn Sonata*".

The distinction between expressive commending and directive recommending is underscored by the fact that, by contrast with *commend,* the illocutionary verb *recommend* has a directive syntax. Admittedly, *recommend* does not as happily co-occur with "*N* to *V* +" nominals as do exemplary directive verbs like *order, advise, exhort,* and so on.

I recommend to you to go to *Autumn Sonata*

is substandard. Even so, *recommend* clearly belongs syntactically with such directive illocutionary verbs. For the more natural explicit performative sentence

I recommend (to you) that you (should) go to *Autumn Sonata*

has the deep structure

I recommend to you + you (should) go to *Autumn Sonata*

which exhibits the characteristic pattern for explicit performative sentences associated with directive verbs.

Summing up: prescriptivism is perhaps most plausible in what it has to say about the meaning of *good* in terms of, specifically, commendatory illocutionary-force potential. This plausibility turns out to be spurious, however, for commendation does not belong among directive, or, in Hare's term, prescriptive, illocutions. It is, rather, an expressive illocution. The classification of commendation as prescriptive, that is, directive, looks like the confusion of commendation with recommendation, which is directive.

IV

If evaluative terms like *good, right, ought,* and so on, build an imperative element into the meaning of the categorical affirmatives that contain them, evaluative illocutions performed in uttering such categorical affirmatives necessarily will be constituted, at least in part, by directive illocutions. But such evaluative illocutions can be entirely dissociated from directive illocutionary force; therefore prescriptivism, even in its sophisticated restatement, is finally untenable. This point, moreover, can be made with respect to those categorical affirmative evaluatives that particularly interest us, namely, those apt for expressing all-out present-tense summary evaluative judgements about action.

It is undisputed that there are speech contexts in which categorical affirmative evaluative illocutions are *in some way* associated with directive illocutions. For example, you ask me to advise you what to do, and I answer, "Very well, you ought to leave at once". Another example, one of unsolicited suggestion, occurs in the following interchange between Abigail and Samuel in Donleavy's *The Saddest Summer of Samuel S.*:

> 'Do you like living primitive like this?'
> 'No.'
> 'Why do you?'
> 'Because I haven't the money to live any other way and nobody else will clean it up.'
> 'You should clean it.'
> 'I don't feel like cleaning it.'
> 'Forgive me for suggesting.'

Another example: you ask me whether I can recommend a movie, and I respond, "Yes. There is one. You would do well to take yourself off to Bergman's *Autumn Sonata*", or "Yes, *Autumn Sonata* is good"; or yet again, you ask me, on someone else's behalf, what advice I have for him, and I say, "No doubt about it. He ought to leave straightaway"; and so on. These examples illustrate that categorical affirmative evaluative illocutions can be connected with varying directive illocutions. The issue, however, is whether disconnection is possible; and I wish to argue, against Hare, that it is.

There is strong syntactic evidence that evaluations, understood as speech-acts,[23] are not intrinsically related to directive illocutions. For verbs like *evaluate, assess, appraise, grade, rank, rate,* and the like (Vendler, *RC*, pp. 29–30, 34), display syntactic affinity with a group of illocutionary verbs which identify as denoting *representative* illocutions, namely, verbs like *call, describe, characterize, diagnose, class, classify, identify,* and so on (*RC*, ch. 2, pp. 19, 34). The characteristic syntax of *evaluate, assess,* and so on, is exhibited by explicit performative sentences like

> I evaluate his work as good
> I assess her effort as fair
> I rank her first

which are comparable to sentences like

> I call it subterfuge
> I describe this book as red
> I diagnose your illness as schizophrenia
> I classify Genet as a poet.

Such explicit performative sentences characteristically have the syntactic form

$$N_i V_i N_j \text{ (as) } N_k/A$$

for which the deep structure is

$$N_i V_i N_j + N_j \text{ is } N_k/A^{24}$$

Now paradigm representative verbs like *state, assert, predict, report, maintain,* etc.,[25] have a different syntax from this. Such verbs characteristically are associated with explicit performative sentences of the form

$$N_i V_i \text{ that N V } +$$

for which the deep structure is

$$N_i V_i + \text{N V} +{}^{26}$$

But there is good reason to collect together

$$N_i V_i \text{ that N V } +$$
$$N_i V_i N_j \text{ (as) } N_k/A$$

as the *two* syntactic forms typical for *representative* illocutionary verbs.

Consider verbs like *call, describe, characterize, diagnose,* and so on. It is a puzzle where the illocutions denoted by these verbs are located in an adequate taxonomy. Austin,[27] for example, puts *call, describe, class,* and *identify* into his expositive camp and includes *describe, characterize,* and *diagnose* as verdictives. For my part, I am impressed by what Searle has to say about the illocutions in question, that there is no semantic division between them and representative illocutions corresponding to the difference in syntax between the verbs that denote them and representative verbs like *state, assert, predict,* and so on. Searle writes:

> Do we require a separate semantic category to account for these syntactical facts? I think not. I think there is a much simpler explanation of the distribution of these verbs. Often, in representative discourse, we focus our attention on some topic of discussion. The question is not just what is the propositional content we are asserting, but what do we say about the *object(s)* referred to in the propositional content: not just what do we state, claim, characterize, or assert, but how do we describe, call, diagnose or identify *it,* some previously referred to topic of discussion. When, for example, there is a question of diagnosing or describing it is always a question of diagnosing a person or his case, of describing a landscape or a party or a person, etc. These Representative illocutionary verbs give us a device for isolating topics from what is said about topics. But this very genuine syntactical difference does not mark a semantic difference big enough to justify the formation of a separate category (CIA, p. 19).[28]

Indeed, as Searle goes on to note in support of his interpretation, we typically call, describe, characterize, and so forth, in issuing utterances that are statements that something is the case; we rarely employ explicit performatives like "I (hereby) describe this book as red", "I (hereby) diagnose your illness as schizophrenia", and the like (p. 20).

To sum up, the situation seems to be like this. There are two characteristic syntactic forms for representative illocutionary verbs. The form associated with verbs like *state, assert,* and so on, reflects the direct focus of our attention on *what is said.* The form associated with verbs like *call, describe,* and so on, reflects the direct focus of our attention on the thing about which what is said is said—the *topic* of discourse.

Illocutionary verbs like *evaluate, assess, grade,* etc., share the characteristic syntax of topic-focused representative verbs like *call, describe, characterize,* etc. This is good reason to think that, semantically, they are themselves topic-focused representative verbs. And indeed, it seems clear what the relation is between verbs like *describe* and *characterize,* on the one hand, and *evaluate* and *assess,* on the other, namely, a relation of general to more specific terms. *Describe* and *characterize,* it would seem, denote illocutions (descriptions, characterizations) of which the illocutions denoted by *evaluate* and *assess* (evaluations, assessments) are species; which, presumably, is the insight expressed by the philosopher's term of art, "desirability characterization".[29] In short, *evaluate* and *assess* appear to be in rather the same classificatory line of business as the obsolete verb *macarize* and the invented verb *rubrify.* (*SA,* p. 70). *Macarize* marks out characterizations in which persons are characterized as happy, and *rubrify* is concocted to pick out characterizations in which things are characterized as red. *Evaluate* and *assess,* for their part, would seem to identify that subclass of characterizations in which things are called desirable or undesirable, good or bad, right or wrong, and so on; or at least something that supports some such characterization.

There is, then, strong syntactic reason for discounting the idea that evaluative illocutions are necessarily associated with, because in part constituted by, directive illocutions. In sum: the corresponding illocutionary verbs have one of the syntaxes characteristic of representative illocutionary verbs. Semantic considerations corroborate the evidence of syntax here. For it is possible to adduce many examples of evaluative illocutions, and, in particular, categorical affirmative illocutions, that are themselves detached from directive illocutions.

Consider, for example, (1)–(5):

(1) You ask me to advise you what to do, but I say: "Well, I don't mind letting you know what I think you should do. You should leave at once. I'm sure of that. But I want you to be clear that when I say this I'm not advis-

ing you, or urging you, or even suggesting to you, to leave at once. Nothing like that. It's really quite up to you what you do."

(2) I say to you: "The right thing for me to do is to leave at once. I know that. But please don't take me as in any way putting it to you to leave at once. I see no point in that. You, no doubt, will do as you see fit, without the least hestitation."

(3) You ask me to recommend a movie, but I say: "Well, *Autumn Sonata* is good. But I'm not prepared to recommend, or even suggest, you go to it. For I'm not sure it's your kind of movie."

(4) You ask me, on Fred's behalf, what advice I have for him on what to do, but I reply: "Well, who am I even to suggest to Fred what to do? He ought to leave straightaway. I'm certain of that. You can tell Fred what I think he should do. But also tell him that it's not for me to say to him what to do. I'll stand by him whatever he decides."

And finally:

(5) You ask me what I think is the right thing for Fred to do, and I say: "Well, I've no doubts about it. The right thing for Fred to do is to leave at once"—adding—"But that's between you and me. You wouldn't catch me dead even suggesting he do this."

There does not seem to be anything the least semantically untoward about the speaker's remarks in (1)–(5), which are naturally interpreted as utterances in which speakers explicitly dissociate their categorical affirmative evaluations from even the mildest relevant directive illocutionary intent. Such remarks dramatically contrast with comments like: "Snow is white, but I'm not saying this is so", "Leave at once, but I'm not saying to you that you (should) do this", "I will leave at once, but I'm not committing myself to doing this", and so on, which are evidently self-contradictory. If this is right, (1)–(5) would seem to defeat the central prescriptivist claim that, as a result of incorporating such terms, categorical affirmatives that include evaluative terms have an imperative-mood element in their meaning. For, if such categoricals did have such a semantical component, evaluative illocutions performed in their literal utterances necessarily would have directive illocutionary force as an aspect of their evaluative illocutionary force; but (1)–(5) above provide counterexamples to that claim.

Perhaps it will be claimed, in prescriptivism's defense, that (1)–(5) are not examples of *genuine* evaluative illocutions, but involve only so-called "inverted comma" △ uses of evaluative terms.[30] This seems, however, entirely gratuitous. It might be conceded, on the other hand, that the examples in question involve *bona fide* evaluative illocutions, and yet one might insist that, insofar as this is so, there is indeed a directive (or prescriptive) element in them which is properly understood as a *general,* although not universal, directive (or prescriptive) illocution.[31] This too seems gratuitous and counterintuitive for the cases under discussion; but, in any case, it seems perfectly possible to construct strengthened examples in which genuine evaluative illocutions are accompanied by explicit dissociation from any such general directive illocutionary intent. For example:

(6) You ask me to advise you what to do, but I say: "Well, I don't mind letting you know what I think you should do. You should leave at once. I'm sure of that. But I want you to be clear that when I say this I'm not advising you, or urging you, or even suggesting to you, to leave at once. Nothing like that. I don't have any interest in saying to anyone, including you, what to do in situations like this. It's really quite up to each person what he does."

(7) I say to you: "The right thing for me to do is to leave at once. I know that. But please don't take me as in any way putting it to you to leave at once. I see no point in saying to anyone what to do in situations like this.

Each person, I'm sure, will do as he sees fit, without the least hesitation."

(8) You ask me to recommend a movie, but I say: "Well, *Autumn Sonata* is good. But I never make recommendations, or even suggestions, to anyone about movies. For I'm never sure that what I think good is their kind of movie."

(9) You ask me, on Fred's behalf, what advice I have for him on what to do, but I reply: "Well, who am I even to suggest to anyone, let alone Fred, what to do in a situation like this? Fred ought to leave straightaway. I'm certain of that. You can tell Fred what I think he should do. But also tell him that it's not for me to say to anyone what to do in such a situation, least of all him. I'll stand by him whatever he decides."

And finally:

(10) You ask me what I think is the right thing for Fred to do, and I say: "Well, I've no doubts about it. The right thing for Fred to do is to leave at once"—adding— "But that's between you and me. You wouldn't catch me dead even suggesting to someone what to do in circumstances like this."

I think that (1)–(5) furnish natural counterexamples to the central prescriptivist claim that, as a result of incorporating such terms, categorical affirmatives that include evaluative terms have an imperative-mood element in their meaning. Perhaps, however, as I have said, this will be objected to on the grounds—to my mind, gratuitous and counterintuitive—that there is a residual general directive (or prescriptive) element in these affirmatives. In this case, I offer (6)–(10) for consideration. The remarks in (6)–(10) seem perfectly intelligible; yet they exhibit relevant evaluative illocutions accompanied by explicit *universal* dissociation by speakers from even the mildest directive illocutionary intent. In short: if not (1)–(5), then (6)–(10) bear adequate witness to the untenability of the central prescriptivist thesis that positive evaluative terms, as a fundamental aspect of their meaning, invest categorical affirmatives that incorporate them with directive (in its term, prescriptive) illocutionary-force potential in the same way that the syntactic forms associated with the imperative mood invest the sentences to which they are attached with such illocutionary-force potential.

V

Some final considerations. Previously I detailed how prescriptivism, at least in its sophisticated restatement, can defend itself against the charge that it unacceptably forces multiplicity of meaning of evaluative terms. It is now time to qualify this sympathetic treatment. For, although prescriptivism is perfectly compatible with evaluative terms' being univocal throughout syntactical transformations of categorical affirmatives like "This is a good x", "I ought to leave at once",[32] and so on, it is *not* compatible with such terms' being univocal throughout their occurrences in *all* categorical affirmatives; this seems unacceptable.

Consider, for example, categorical affirmatives like:

(i)   You ought to believe she is lying (it's staring you in the face)

(ii) You ought to feel ashamed (you know how much that would hurt her)

(iii) It's good/right to desire such things

(iv) There ought to be less suffering in the world (too few have the chance to be happy)

(v)   Fred ought to try to kill him tonight (that's what I make of the evidence to hand).

Evaluative illocutions performed in uttering sentences like (i)–(v) can have directive illocutionary associations. For example, someone who says to another, "You ought to believe she is lying;

it's staring you in the face", might well, on occasion, be correctly described as, *inter alia*, urging or exhorting that person to reconsider the evidence. Or again, take (iv). Utterances of (iv) are naturally associated with expressions of wishes like, "Would that there were less suffering in the world!" But they can also be associated with directives. One might, for example, say something like (iv) in order to urge, or exhort, or request another to stay his hand against someone. It is equally evident, however, that (i)–(v) will not support the claim that the evaluative words occurring in them function semantically as imperative-mood signs. The verbs within the scopes of the evaluative terms in (i)–(iv) do not tolerate imperativisation, for they are not verbs of action[33]; and (v), inasmuch as it is about what is probable, is revealed as semantically ineligible to have an imperative with *try* as its principal verb as part of its meaning.

(i)–(v), then, represent examples of categorical affirmatives which incorporate evaluative terms but which cannot intelligibly be credited with imperative-mood meaning. The prescriptivist, it seems, will be forced to say, in the end, that evaluative terms do not mean the same when they occur in sentences like (i)–(v) as they do when they co-occur with verbs of action in categoricals like "You ought to leave at once (decency requires it)", and so on, or when they occur in certain favoured categoricals[34] like "This is a good strawberry (motorcar, movie)". But this is an entirely unhappy result. For there is every reason to think that evaluative terms are univocal throughout their occurrences in such sentences.

Consider, for example, that it is in principle possible to generate sentences like

(vi)   You ought (both) to believe she is lying and to confront her with her deceit (cf. (i))

(vii) You ought (both) to feel ashamed and to apologize at once (cf. (ii))

(viii) It's good/right (both) to desire such things and to tell others that one does (cf. (iii)) and, more awkwardly,

> (ix) There ought (both) to be less suffering in the world and as much as possible done by all of us to wipe it out (cf. (iv))

in which evaluative terms have mixed scopes which include verbs of action.

(vi)–(ix) attest to the fact that evaluative terms do not change their meaning in such sentential environments depending upon whether their scopes incorporate verbs of action. For it is a semantic condition on the generation of each of (vi)–(ix) that the evaluative terms in them have one and the same meaning with respect to each of the conjuncts occurring within their scopes. (v) introduces an especially interesting case. Many philosophers have wanted to contend that *ought* has a distinct sense in probability examples like (v).[35] Now there certainly is an important semantic difference between *ought*-sentences like (i), (ii), and (iv) and *ought*-sentences like (v). This is a difference to which A. R. White has drawn attention in *Modal Thinking*.[36] In (i), (ii), and (iv), *ought* is subjunctive-governing. Thus, these examples may be rendered as:

> (i)′ It ought to be that you (should) believe she is lying
> (ii)′ It ought to be that you (should) feel ashamed
> (iv)′ It ought to be that there (should) be less suffering in the world

respectively. In (v), by contrast, *ought* is indicative-governing. Thus (v) is rendered as

> (v)′ It ought to be that Fred will try to kill him tonight.

But adequate warrant for thinking that *ought* means the same when indicative-governing as when subjunctive-governing—and, in particular, subjunctive-governing with respect to verbs of action—is the fact that we can form perfectly coherent, though admittedly unfamiliar, sentences like

> (x)   It ought to be that Fred will try to kill him tonight, and hence, that you should take measures to protect him without delay

which depend for their generation on *ought* being univocal with respect to each of the conjuncts, indicative and subjunctive, within its scope.

Summing up: the central tenet of prescriptivism is that it is a fundamental aspect of the meaning of positive evaluative terms that they invest categorical affirmatives containing them with an imperative-mood element in their meaning. Such evaluative terms, as they occur in examples like (i)-(v), however, cannot be reckoned to have this effect on the relevant categoricals. The prescriptivist, it seems, will have to claim that evaluative terms as they occur in (i)-(v) do not mean the same as when they co-occur with verbs of action in categorical affirmatives like "You ought (subjunctive) to leave at once", "It's good/right to do *x*", and so on, or when they occur in certain favoured categorical affirmatives like "This is a good movie", and so forth. The prescriptivist, it seems, will have to claim that prescriptivism's specific concern is with what evaluative terms mean as they occur in the latter sentences and their syntactical transformations. My objection here has been that the examples (vi)-(x) indicate that evaluative terms *do* mean the same in categorical affirmatives like (i)-(v) as they do in prescriptivism's counterpart favoured examples. I conclude that, as became evident in Section 4 in connection with those examples, prescriptivism must, here too, pay the price for having articulated an account of the meaning of evaluative terms under bewitchment from a certain slender diet of uses of evaluative categoricals, namely, that range of uses which is located, in Roger Wertheimer's words, "at the nexus of argument and action" (*Significance of Sense*, ch. 1, p. 27).[37]

VI

Hare thinks that, because they incorporate evaluative terms, evaluatives apt for expressing all-out present-tense summary evaluative judgements about action are partially imperatival, and that, insofar as this is the case, the corresponding evaluative thinking is revealed as partially volitional. In the next chapter, I wish to argue that imperativity is, in any case, an unsuitable semantic feature to mark an intrinsic relation between evaluative thinking about one's own action and volitions *to act*. But the argument of the present chapter has been, in effect, that the evaluatives in question do not contain an imperative semantical component and hence do not in this way indicate the partially volitional character of the relevant evaluative thinking. The volitionist idea that there is a logically necessary *because intrinsic* connection between such evaluative thinking as characterizes the putative akrates and the presence in him of some corresponding volition, perhaps even intention, to act cannot be grounded in the partial imperativity of the language apt for expressing all-out present-tense summary evaluative thinking about action, because, quite simply, the language in question is *not*, even in part, imperatival.

CHAPTER THREE

Evaluatives, Volitives, Indicatives, and Evaluative Thinking

HARE'S VOLITIONISM fails to respect certain differences within the language apt for expressing volitions about future action. It now becomes important to specify what these differences are. Hare thinks that first-person singular imperatives are suitable sentences for expressing in words what we are thinking when we have volitions to act. This is why he thinks that universally prescriptive all-out present-tense summary evaluative thinking about one's own action is revealed as partially constituted by a consonant volition to act, inasmuch as the evaluatives corresponding to such thinking contain first-person singular imperatives. In the present chapter, I want to argue, first, that it is a mistake to think that volitions to act are thus expressible as (first-person singular) imperatives; and second, that evaluatives apt for putting into words all-out present-tense summary evaluative thinking about one's own action (or, indeed, someone else's) do not semantically incorporate such volitive sentences as are appropriate for expressing volitions to act, namely, *intentives* (in the case of intentions to act) and *conatives* (in the case of mere desires to act). Such evaluatives, I contend, do not include any relevant volitive-mood element in their meaning (that is, any imperative, intentive, or conative element), but are *only* what they unquestionably are, namely, indicatives; and correspondingly, the evaluative thinking such evaluatives are suitable for expressing is *only* what it undeniably is, namely, cognitive or theoretical thinking. This will complete my argument that there is no logically necessary *because constitutive* relation between such evaluative thinking as characterizes the putative akrates and the presence on his part of some corresponding volition to act.

I

Hare's view that first-person singular imperatives are appropriate sentences in which to express what we are thinking when we have volitions to act is part of the more general view that imperatives are suitable sentences in which to express what we are thinking when we have volitions about future action, our own or others'. For brevity, I shall refer to this view as the imperative theory of the will (ITW).[1] The question now is: Why does Hare embrace ITW?

In *The Language of Morals* and *Freedom and Reason*, the underlying intuition appears to be that imperatives are privileged as basic and direct answers to practical questions of what to do.[2] As far as I am aware, it is in his 1971 paper, "Wanting: Some Pitfalls", that Hare's most extended defense of ITW occurs.[3] There he appears to offer two main positive arguments in its support. In the first, he begins by discussing a subjunctive-employing equivalent of the sentence "X wants (to have) sugar in his soup", namely, "X wants that he have sugar in his soup". Hare writes:

> Here the subordinate *oratio obliqua* clause "that he have sugar in his soup" stands for what in *oratio recta* would be an imperative; if we were translating "wants that he have sugar in his soup" into Urdu, the construction used would be that appropriate to an indirect command. And indeed, in Urdu, as in English, if we are reporting in indirect speech a command given by somebody else, we may say to the person commanded "So and so *wants* you to do such and such". So there is good reason for allowing that, whether or not the man who wants something "says anything in his heart", an appropriate expression in language for what he is thinking, if we are to have one, is an imperative (p. 85).[4]

The second argument runs thus:

> Actually it is very plausible to say that when Hannibal orders his troops to march on Rome he is not merely com-

manding them to do so, but expressing the intention that they should do so; and this lends some plausibility to the thesis that when I form the intention to go to Rome, I have that in mind which would, if expressed in words, naturally be expressed by saying "Let me go to Rome", or if I were to address myself in military style in the mood which I was taught in the Army to call the future imperative, "Hare will go to Rome", or "I will go to Rome" (p. 94).

Consider the first argument here. Even if the nominals that depend on *want* are indirect commands, that is, syntactic structures that reproduce in *oratio obliqua* what in *oratio recta* would be imperatives, this would not itself be good reason to think that imperatives are appropriate expressions in language for what we are thinking when we want to do something or when we want someone else to do something. For consider the sentences:

    (1) N believes that p
    (2) N hopes that p
    (3) N fears that p
    (4) N is ashamed that p
    (5) N is glad that p
    (6) N is pleased that p
    (7) N regrets that p
    (8) N is proud that p.

In (1)–(8) the subordinate nominals are indirect *statements*, that is, syntactic structures that reproduce in *oratio obliqua* what in *oratio recta* would be indicatives. However, although indicatives are suitable independent sentences in which to express what we are thinking when we believe something, they are not suitable independent sentences in which to express what we are thinking when we hope for, fear, are ashamed of, are glad about or pleased at, regret or are proud of, something. What makes indicatives appropriate independent sentences in which to express (that is, formulate, put, set forth, represent, and so on) in words what we are thinking when we believe something is that indicatives are semantically associated, via their indicativity, with representative illocutions that correspond in content to what they express in *oratio rec-*

ta; and such representative illocutions, in turn, count as expressions (that is, manifestations) of *beliefs* to the same effect. This is so because believing that something is the case is the sincerity condition on saying that it is.[5]

Similarly, whether independent imperatives are appropriate sentences in which to express what we are thinking when we intend or want to do something or intend or want someone else to do something, is, at heart, a question of whether directive illocutions, the illocutions with which imperatives are semantically associated, count as expressions (that is, manifestations) of such intentions or desires. For, if they do so count, we will be able to say something like the following. What makes imperatives appropriate sentences in which to express in words what we are thinking when we intend or want to do something or intend or want that someone else should do something, is that imperatives are semantically associated, via their imperativity, with directive illocutions that correspond in content to what they express in *oratio recta;* and such directive illocutions, in turn, count as expressions of intentions or desires to the same effect. Whether this is so is a question of whether having such intentions or desires about the future actions of oneself or others constitutes the sincerity condition on issuing directives.

Hare, for his part, is not insensitive to these considerations. For the second segment of his first argument lays stress on the fact that directive illocutions are reportable by saying things like "So and so *wants* you to do such and such", and the gist of his second argument for ITW seems to be that support for ITW, particularly in relation to intentions to act, derives from the fact that a specific directive illocution, such as an order, counts not merely as a command (Hare's generic term in "Wanting" [pp. 95 ff] for what I prefer to call a directive) but also as an expression of a corresponding intention.

Now it is of course true that directive illocutions, the illocutions with which imperatives are semantically connected, count as the expression of certain intentions or desires, and so independent imperatives are correctly identified as appropriate sentences in which to express such volitions. But what Hare ignores is that directive illocutions are essentially illocutions in which one person says to someone *else* that he should do something and therefore count as expressing intentions or desires on the part of speakers that *others* should act in certain ways,[6] given that it is a sincerity condition on such illocutions that such other-person intentions or desires are present in speakers (Searle, *SA* 3.4, p. 65; CIA, p.4). Thus, although it is correct that imperatives are suitable sentences in which to express certain intentions or desires, those intentions or desires do not include intentions or desires to do something *oneself:* they include, rather, only intentions or desires that someone *else* should do something. Hare is impressed by the role of imperatives as answers to practical questions of what to do. But the critical point he misses is this: imperatives are appropriate as answers to such questions only from the point of view of someone *other* than the person for whom the question arises in the first person.[7]

What about *self-addressed* directive illocutions? In my opinion, *typical so-called* self-addressed directive illocutions do not impugn the view that *bona fide* directives are essentially other-oriented. For these utterances, I suggest, are not themselves *bona fide* or serious directives: rather, they represent self-dissociative exercises of the imagination in which individuals imagine that they are issuing directives to someone *else* (or that one part of themselves is issuing directives to a *different* part of themselves, or some such; cf. Hare, *FR* 5.8, p. 81) in order to get *themselves* to act in certain ways.[8] The grammatical person of the imperatives used for such purposes (usually second-person singular) is especially noteworthy here. Below is a selection of examples.

In book 8, chapter 11, of *The Confessions,* Augustine writes:

> And [Continence] smiled on me with a persuasive mockery, as would she say, ''. . . Cast thyself upon Him, fear not, He will not withdraw Himself that thou shouldest fall; cast thyself fearlessly upon Him, He will receive and will heal thee'' . . . And she again seemed to say, ''Stop thine ears against *those* thy unclean *members on the earth,* that they may be *mortified. They tell thee of delights, but not as doth the law of the Lord thy God.''* This controversy in my heart was self against self only.[9]

In the short story *The Lovely Lady*, D. H. Lawrence writes:

> When suddenly out of the hole came a sigh and a last whisper. 'Ah, well! Pauline! Get up, it's enough for today!' Good God! Out of the hole of the rain-pipe! The rain-pipe was acting as a speaking-tube! Impossible! No, quite possible. She had read of it even in some book. And Aunt Pauline, like the old and guilty woman she was, talked aloud to herself. That was it![10]

In *Seize the Day*, Saul Bellow writes:

> Yes, it was age. Don't make an issue of it, Wilhelm advised himself. If you were to ask the old doctor in what year he had interned, he'd tell you correctly. All the same, don't make an issue. Don't quarrel with your own father. Have pity on an old man's failings (p. 32).

And again:

> Moreover, he advised himself repeatedly not to discuss his vexatious problems with him, for his father, with some justice, wanted to be left in peace. Wilhelm also knew that when he began to talk about these things he made himself feel worse, he became congested with them and worked himself into a clutch. Therefore he warned himself, lay off, pal. It'll only be an aggravation. From a deeper source, however, came other promptings (p. 48).

And later:

> Again Wilhelm cautioned himself. Remember his age (p. 57).

Finally, many excellent examples occur in Ernest Hemingway's *The Old Man and the Sea*. Thus:

> I wish he'd sleep and I could sleep and dream about lions, he thought. Why are the lions the main thing that is left?

> Don't think, old man, he said to himself. Rest gently now against the wood and think of nothing. He is working. Work as little as you can (p. 62).

And again:

> But remember to sleep, he thought. Make yourself do it and devise some simple and sure way about the lines. Now go back and prepare the dolphin. It is too dangerous to rig the oars as a drag if you must sleep. I could go without sleeping, he told himself. But it would be too dangerous (p. 72).

And in yet another place there is this gem:

> Now, he said to himself. Look to the lashing on the knife and see if it has been cut. Then get your hand in order because there still is one to come. 'I wish I had a stone for the knife', the old man said after he had checked the lashing on the oar butt. 'I should have brought a stone'. You should have brought many things, he thought. But you did not bring them, old man. Now is no time to think of what you do not have. Think of what you can do with what there is.
>
> 'You give me much good counsel', he said aloud. 'I'm tired of it' (p. 103).[11]

Such putative examples of self-addressed directive illocutions are, I suggest, merely *simulacra* of interpersonal directives, and thus do *not* challenge the view that *bona fide* directives are essentially other-oriented. Indeed, so interpreted, such examples only serve to underscore the other-orientedness of their *bona fide* models. And this feature of other-orientedness, I contend, is the fundamental fact about *bona fide* directive illocutions which defeats the suggestion that imperatives are appropriate sentences in which to express what we are thinking when we intend or desire *to do* something. For, insofar as directives, the illocutions with which imperatives are semantically associated, are other-oriented, they count, by virtue of the sincerity-condition relation, only as expressions of corresponding intentions or desires that someone *else* should do something.[12]

It is, indeed, *commissive*, and not directive, illocutions that are connected with *intentions* to act via the sincerity-condition relation. That is, it is saying as a commitment (a promise, undertaking, offer, pledge, vow, guarantee, or the like) that one will do something which counts as expressing a corresponding intention to act, given that so intending is the sincerity condition on issuing such a self-commitment to action. Hare's proposal that (first-person singular) imperatives are appropriate sentences in which to express what we are thinking when we intend to act relies on the assimilation at one point—namely, where one answers in the first person a practical question of what to do—of directive and commissive illocutionary force. Hare, for his part, explicitly embraces this assimilation. Thus in *The Language of Morals*, at 2.2, he declares: "In the case of first-person commands ('Let me do so and so') and resolves ('I will do so and so'), which are closely similar to one another, affirmation and assent are identical" (*LM* 2.2, p. 20); and in *Freedom and Reason*, at 5.6, he remarks: "While continuing to prescribe that everyone *else* (or at any rate everyone whose interests do not especially concern us) should act in accordance with the principle, we do not so prescribe to ourselves (for to do this fully and in earnest would commit us to acting)" (*FR* 5.6, p. 76).

But it is incoherent that directive and commissive illocutionary force should in this way coalesce. The category division here is unbridgeable; and the idea of a (first-person singular) imperative with commissive illocutionary-force potential is a semantical solecism. For, quite simply, commissive and directive illocutions belong to complementary dialectical slots: the former (in which speakers commit themselves to act in certain ways) are semantically suited to serve as *answers* or *replies*, positive or negative, to the latter (in which speakers say or put it to hearers that they [should] act in certain ways).[13] It might well be of course that on occasion, to adapt a line from Augustine,[14] such readiness is there that directive (or simulated directive) is scarcely distinct from corresponding commissive; but this does not speak to the semantical relation between them, which keeps them categorically separate and specifies that the commissives are appropriate for *answering* directives.

Hare is adamant that directive illocutions (in his terms, prescriptions, or commands, or imperations)[15] are not essentially attempts by speakers to get hearers to act in certain ways. This, he charges, confuses illocutions with perlocutions.[16] According to Hare, what I am calling directive illocutions simply are, in essence, illocutions in which a speaker *tells* or *prescribes* to someone (possibly himself) what to do: provides *guidance* to someone (possibly himself) on what to do.[17] The point is interesting. For Hare is sensitive to the fact that utterances of expressions of intention to act cannot be construed as attempts by speakers to get hearers to act in certain ways. In defense (against Pears) of Kenny's view that intentions are sayings-in-the-heart of commands,[18] for example, he effectively accepts the point that such directive illocutionary force as attaches to utterances of putative expressions of intention like "Let me do x" cannot be exhortative, because (according to him) exhortation is, at least partly, "an act of trying to get" ("Wanting", pp. 91–94).

Now the position that directive illocutions characteristically are, *one and all*, attempts by speakers to get addressees to act in certain ways[19] seems patently false. Surely only *sincere* directives are like this.[20] But against Hare there are these points to be made. First, the characterization of directives as attempts to get people to act in certain ways does *not* confuse illocutions with perlocutions. For such a characterization simply represents a *re*characterization of these *il*locutions as *per*locutionary attempts (cf. Searle, CIA, p. 3). Second, even in terms of Hare's preferred essential characterization of directive illocutions (which is, in fact, too specific to be acceptable as a generic characterization), it seems very clear that directives and commissives are quite distinct and that the relation between them is that the latter are appropriate for responding to the former. For surely telling someone to do something is one thing, and his committing himself to doing it is quite another, and the relation between the two is that the latter is appropriate for answering the former in the affirmative.

Summing up so far: Hare contends that (first-person singular) imperatives are suitable sentences for expressing in words what we are thinking when we have volitions *to act*. The crucial issue here is whether directive illocutions, the illocutions with which imperatives are semantically associated, ever count as expressing such volitions. The answer to this, I contend, is no. For directive illocutions are essentially *other*-oriented and hence, always count only as expressions of intentions or desires that *others* should act in certain ways (but see fn. 12 above). Typical cases of the phenomena that go by the name of self-addressed directives reflect this fundamental fact about *bona fide* directive illocutions. For they, I suggest, are imitative of the latter as self-dissociative exercises of the imagination in which individuals imagine that they are issuing directives to someone *else*, in order to get themselves to act in certain ways. Imperatives, in consequence, are apt only for putting into words what we are thinking when we have *other*-person intentions or desires about future action (but, again, see fn. 12). In fact, so far at least as *intentions* to act are concerned, it is commissive, not directive, illocutions that are connected with volitions *to act* via the sincerity-condition relation. Hare's idea that (first-person singular) imperatives are appropriate sentences for expressing intentions to act turns on the assimilation of commissive to directive illocutionary force in the case of first-person answers to practical questions of what to do. But these illocutionary forces are semantically barred from such fusion: commissive illocutions belong at the "receiving end"[21] of relevant directive illocutions as *answers* to them.

II

The question now is: What are the sentences apt for putting into words what we are thinking when we intend or desire to do something? Consider, first, the case where we intend to act. Intentions to act, I have said, are connected with commissive illocutions via the sincerity-condition relation: when we promise, undertake, offer, etc.,[22] to do something we count as expressing (that is, manifesting) an intention so to act, given that the presence of such an intention is the sincerity condition on our so committing ourselves (see Searle, *SA* 3.4, p. 65; CIA, p. 4). So the focus becomes: Are there sentences semantically linked to commissive illocutions in the way indicatives and imperatives are semantically linked, respectively, to representative and directive illocutions? For, if there are, we will be able to say something like this: such *intentives* are appropriate independent sentences in which to express what we are thinking when we have intentions to act because they are semantically associated, via their intentivity, with commissive illocutions that correspond in content to what they express in *oratio recta;* and such commissive illocutions, in turn, count as expressions of intentions to act to the same effect.

It would seem that a sentence like "I will (shall) do *x*" is the prime candidate to be reckoned as sometimes an intentive, that is, as sometimes having it as part of its meaning (the part that relates to the syntactic form of its main verb) that its literal utterance would be, in an appropriate context, a case of committing oneself to doing *x*. Such a sentence, we know, cannot, *pace* Hare, be an imperative: in virtue of its other-orientedness imperativity rejects the first-person singular. But it can be a future indicative: I can, for example, predict what I will (shall) do. Indeed, it appears there can be grammatical indications as to whether such a sentence is an intentive or an indicative. In *Words and Deeds*, David Holdcroft (who uses *commissive* where I prefer *intentive*) comments:

> If it is prefixed by certain sentence adverbs, for example, 'probably' and 'possibly', then it is unambiguously an indicative, whilst if it is followed by 'without fail' it is unambiguously a commissive. Secondly, as Palmer points out, 'Mary will not be met by me at the station' is not the passive of the commissive 'I will not meet Mary at the station'; though it is the passive of the indicative 'It will not be the case that I meet Mary at the station' (ch. 7, p. 120).

It is even a convention in some quarters (which I shall not follow) to use "I will do *x*" as an intentive and "I shall do *x*" as an indicative; or at any rate, less committally, "I will" where there is, as Fowler's *Modern English Usage* puts it, "an implication of intention, volition, or choice".[23]

The scene is set, however, for contention among philosophers as to whether "I will (shall) do *x*" ever has intentive, or at least purely intentive, occurrences. For example, in *Freedom of the Individual*, Stuart Hampshire writes:

> The statement 'I shall come to the meeting' has therefore a double aspect, and is subject to at least two criteria, or tests, of correctness: first, is it a reliable guide to the future, and, secondly, is the intention announced a misguided or a confused one? (ch. 3, pp. 72–73).

In like vein, David Pears comments in the paper "Predicting and Deciding":

> To say, 'I will do *A*' is, on any view, to hold up a rather complex target. If someone retorts 'You will not in fact do *A* (although you intend to)', that will hit the target. If he retorts 'You do not intend to do *A*', that too will hit the target. How should we characterize these two impacts? The simplest answer to this question is that the target is a conjunction, and that each retort is the contradictory of one of its members. If that answer were right, the contradictory rejoinder would be the disjunction of the two retorts, and the complete denial would be the conjunction of them. However, there are reasons for regarding this simple answer as too crude. I shall not explore these reasons, or try to refine on the answer. But, if what I have been saying is right, any refinement of it must allow the first retort to be characterized as the imputation of some kind of mistake in what was said. This does not require that the first retort should be the contradictory rejoinder (p. 30).

Pears reiterates this theme in his reply to Hare's "Wanting" paper.[24] For Pears, very clearly, the problem is, specifically, the extent to which "I will (shall) do *A*" is a *statement that one intends* to do *A* and the extent to which it is a *prediction that one will* do *A*.[25]

John Searle, for his part, treats sentences like "I will (shall) do *x*" as simply future indicatives in the literal utterances of which we sometimes perform *indirect* commissives by making future-tense statements.[26] For Searle, there is a directive parallel here in connection with sentences like ''Officers will henceforth wear ties at dinner''. Such sentences, he thinks, are future indicatives in the literal utterances of which we sometimes perform *indirect* directives by making future-tense statements (pp. 64 ff). Brian O'Shaughnessy adopts a somewhat similar position to this in *The Will*. O'Shaughnessy sums up matters, as he sees them, this way:

> In short, when usually I intend, and let you know of the fact that I intend, I normally do so without mentioning the intention. I normally do so merely by predicting one of my own actions (p. 34).

Philosophers like Hare and Von Wright provide a contrast to the above authors. For Hare there is no question: in certain of its occurrences ''I will do x'' is not any kind of *statement*, but rather an *expression of* an intention or resolve (although he spoils this insight by classifying it as an imperative; ''Wanting'', pp. 94–95). Von Wright, for his part, in commenting on the following argument,

> I intend to make it true that E
> Unless I do A, I shall not achieve this
> Therefore I will do A

writes:

> The conclusion of the first person inference, we said, is a declaration of intention . . . I said there was a ''kind of'' logical connection here. For, although I think it obvious that the conclusion of our first person argument follows logically from the premises, this ''following'' has a peculiar nature: A declaration of intention is not a true or false proposition (''On So-called Practical Inference'', pp. 41, 44–45).

I think that a powerful argument for the view that sentences like ''I will (shall) do x'' have exclusively intentive occurrences can be developed along the following lines. Consider Searle's directive example. According to Searle, we have the following generalization about one of the ways speakers can perform indirect directives:

> Generalization 2: S can make an indirect directive by either asking whether or stating that the propositional content condition obtains (ISA, p. 72).[27]

For example: S can indirectly order officers henceforth to wear ties at dinner (primary illocution) by stating that officers henceforth will wear ties at dinner (secondary illocution) (ISA, Group 3, p. 65). In such a case the uttered sentence counts as a future indicative.

But suppose S were to use an explicit performative sentence to give this order. Then a paradigm sentence for S to utter would be

> I (hereby) order officers henceforth to wear ties at dinner.

Such a sentence, as we have seen, is a nominal compound derived from the elements

> I (hereby) order officers + officers will/shall (should) henceforth wear ties at dinner.

Now the *subjunctive* matrix element here corresponds to appropriate *imperative* primary performative sentences,[28] which is good reason to think that when a speaker S issues an order in uttering so morphemically similar a sentence as

> Officers will (shall) henceforth wear ties at dinner

that sentence itself represents one such *imperative* primary performative. In such a case, what clearly happens is that S *directly* issues an order in the literal utterance of this imperative. In this way, I suggest, it becomes evident that sentences like "Officers will (shall) henceforth wear ties at dinner" are modally versatile: sometimes they are not future indicatives at all, but are imperatives, apt for directly performing directive illocutions.

An analogous argument can be developed to show that sentences like "I will (shall) do *x*" have purely intentive occurrences. According to Searle, there is, among others, the following generalization for indirect commissives:

> Generalization 7: *S* can make an indirect commissive by stating that, and in some forms by asking whether, the propositional content condition obtains (ISA, p. 81; see also p. 71).

For example: *S* can indirectly offer to do *x* for someone (primary illocution) by stating that he will do it for him (secondary illocution) (ISA, Group 3, p. 80). In such a case the uttered sentence counts as a future indicative.

Well, again, there is this line to pursue. Suppose *S* were to use an explicit performative sentence to make this offer. Then a paradigm sentence for *S* to utter would be

I (hereby) offer to do *x* for you.

Such a sentence is the surface structure realization of the elements

I (hereby) offer + I will (shall) do *x* for you

in line with the nominalizing transformation[29]

$$N_i V_i + N_i \text{ subj } (V_j) + \rightarrow N_i V_i \text{ to } V_j +$$

Now the *subjunctive* matrix element here corresponds to appropriate *subjunctive* primary performative sentences. This is the heart of the matter. For surely this is good reason to think that when a speaker *S* issues an offer in uttering a morphemically indistinguishable sentence like

I will (shall) do *x* for you

that sentence itself represents just such a *subjunctive* primary performative. Clearly, what happens, in such a case, is that S *directly* makes his offer in the literal utterance of this subjunctive.

In this way, I suggest, it becomes evident that sentences of the grammatical form of "I will (shall) do *x*" are also modally versatile: sometimes they are not future indicatives at all, but are subjunctives, apt for directly performing commissive illocutions. Such subjunctives, I submit, are *intentives*, that is, subjunctives of the will (volitives) which have it as part of their meaning that their literal utterances would be, in the absence of contextual countersigns, cases of committing oneself to acting in certain ways. *Pace* Hare, it is such intentives issued as self-commitments to action, and not imperatives issued as directives, which are appropriate as direct and basic answers to practical questions of what to do from the point of view of the agent for whom the question arises in the first person.[30]

What then of sentences of the form "Let me do *x*"? Hare appears to favour these as appropriate first-person singular *imperatives* for expressing in words what we are thinking when we have volitions to act.[31] I submit that such "Let me" sentences are less familiar *intentives*, equivalent in meaning to more familiar ones like "I will (shall) do *x*". There is a nice example of the "Let me" construction as intentive in the following passage from *The Old Man and the Sea:*

> 'He is tiring or he is resting', the old man said. 'Now let me get through the eating of this dolphin and get some rest and a little sleep' (p. 74).

As might be expected, "Let me" intentives also occur in rather less recent literary works. For example, in John Donne's "A Nocturnall upon S. Lucies Day, Being the shortest day", we find:

> Since shee enjoys her long nights festivall,
> Let mee prepare towards her, and let mee call
> This houre her Vigill, and her Eve, since this
> Both the yeares, and the dayes deep midnight is.[32]

In his response to Hare's "Wanting" paper, Pears declares:

> Now anyone who utters S4 ('I shall do A'') to someone else, whatever else he does, conveys two pieces of information, the information that he intends to do A, and the information that he will in fact do A. It is true that the exact analysis of S4 is a difficult matter. But, fortunately, it is not necessary for me to try to determine which of the two pieces of information is the main burden of the communication, e.g., whether both facts are asserted, or one is in some way implied, etc. The only point that I need to make here is that the second piece of information is not cancellable - e.g., the speaker of S4 could not cancel it by continuing, ". . . but, in fact, A is impossible." He could not even mitigate it by reducing the categorical force of this part of his communication, e.g., by the continuation, ". . . but, as a matter of fact, I probably shall not be able to do A''. So it seems to me that, whenever someone utters S4, it will not be correct unless it fits his future performance ("Comments'', p. 122).

Pears offers similar observations for "I will do *A*'' (S3 in his discussion; pp. 113–14, 123–24). These remarks are of a piece with those earlier quoted from his paper "Predicting and Deciding''.

I want to stress the following: on a construal of "I will (shall) do *x*'' as *simply an intentive* it is possible to diagnose the oddity of saying such things as "I will (shall) do *x*, but I don't intend to do it'' and "I will (shall) do *x*, but I (probably) will (shall) not be able to do it''. Saying something like the first is reminiscent of Moore's paradox, namely, saying something like "Snow is white, but I don't believe it is''. In such cases, the illocutionary paradox arises out of the fact that the speaker conjoins the performance of an illocution with the denial of the presence of the expressed psychological attitude, which presence is the sincerity condition on the performance of that illocution. What's wrong with saying something like the second is that the speaker conjoins the giving of a commitment to do something with the denial of his ability to keep it. This contrasts with saying something like "I intend to do

x, but I probably shall not be able to do it". For merely to say that one intends to do something can fall short of (indirectly) committing oneself to doing it. What one cannot say here is "I intend to do x, but I shall not be able to do it". For intending to do something presupposes the belief that one will have some chance of being able to do it (some chance of success upon trying).[33]

Similarly, on a construal of "I will (shall) do x" as simply an intentive, it is possible to account for why, as Pears says, if someone says "I will (shall) do x", both "You will not do x (although you intend to)" and "You do not intend to do x" have application as counterrejoinders. Quite simply: the first remark claims that the speaker will not do what he has *committed himself* to doing, although it concedes the sincerity of his self-commitment; whereas the second retort charges the speaker with insincerity.

Finally, Hare, we know, thinks that the nominals in sentences like

> N intends M to do x
> N intends to do x

are indirect *commands*. This is part of what he would appeal to in defense of the view that imperatives are appropriate sentences in which to express what we are thinking when we intend someone else to do something, or to do something ourselves. We are now in a position to correct Hare's interpretation of these noun clauses. In examples like "N intends M to do x", the nominals in queston are indirect commands like the nominals of similar syntactic shape (characteristically "N to V +") that follow directive verbs: they reproduce in *oratio obliqua* what in *oratio recta* would be imperative subjunctives of the will. In examples like "N intends to do x", however, the relevant nominals are indirect *commissives* like the nominals of similar syntactic shape (characteristically "to V +") that follow commissive verbs: they reproduce in *oratio obliqua* what in *oratio recta* would be intentive subjunctives of the will. Nominal compounds like

> N intends M to do x
> N orders M to do x

and

> N intends to do x
>
> N promises to do x

are generated according to these different nominalizations

$$N_i V_i N_j + N_j \text{ subj } (V_j) + \rightarrow N_i V_i N_j \text{ to } V_j +$$
$$N_i V_i + N_i \text{ subj } (V_j) + \rightarrow N_i V_i \text{ to } V_j +$$

respectively. The critical difference here is this: the first transformation depends upon a noun-sharing between the indirect *object* of the container and the subject of the matrix, whereas the second transformation depends upon a noun-sharing between the *subject* of the container and the subject of the matrix.[34]

Directive illocutions, the illocutions with which imperatives are semantically connected, count as expressions of either corresponding intentions or mere desires that others should act in certain ways. Exactly which other-person volition a specific directive counts as expressing seems to depend on the degree of strength with which the directive illocutionary point is presented in that kind of directive. For example: ordering someone to do something seems to be correlated with intending him to, whereas asking someone to do something seems to be correlated with merely wanting him to. But, in any case, we have this result: imperatives, the sentences semantically associated with directive illocutions, are appropriate for expressing in words intentions *and* desires about the future actions of others. But the situation is different in the case of intentives. For commissive illocutions, the illocutions with which intentives are semantically associated, count as expressions of intentions to act, not of mere desires to act; although, of course, intentions to act logically imply corresponding desires. Thus intentives are sentences appropriate for expressing in words only *intentions* to act. It is therefore a question: What about mere desires to act? What are appropriate sentences in which to express what we are thinking when we merely desire to do something?

Usually, it seems, we linguistically express (that is, manifest) our desires to act by issuing self-ascriptions or self-reports like "I want (desire) to do x". This is comparable with the indirect expression of other psychological attitudes by saying things like: "I intend to do x", "I believe that such and such is the case", "I wonder whether such and such is the case", and so forth.[35] In such cases as these, however, it is also available to us to indicate the relevant attitudes in utterances of independent sentences that are suitable for formulating in words what we are thinking when we have such attitudes. For example: in the case of intending to act, there is the intentive "I will (shall) do x"; in the case of intending or wanting you to act, there is the imperative "(You) do x"; in the case of believing that such and such is so, we have the indicative "Such and such is the case"; and, in the case of wondering whether such and such is so, there is the interrogative "Is such and such the case?" The present question is whether there are available to us comparable independent sentences for mere desires to act.

I am impressed by David Gauthier's suggestion that sentences like "I would do x" are suitable for expressing in words what we are thinking when we merely desire to do something.[36] Such sentences appear to be naturally construed as *conatives*, that is, as sentences that have it as part of their meaning, the part that is related to the syntactic form of their principal verbs, that their literal utterances characteristically are expressions (that is, manifestations) of corresponding desires to act (a subclass of expressive illocutions). Such conatives contrast with volitive sentences such as "Would that I had not done x!" *Optatives* like these are suitable for expressing in words what we are thinking when we have "*idle* wishes" about *faits accomplis*; for, as conatives are directly semantically associated with expressing (that is, manifesting) corresponding desires to act, such optatives are directly semantically associated with expressing such corresponding wishes (another subclass of expressive illocutions) (cf. Hare, "Wanting", pp. 89–90).

Putting together the results of sections 1 and 2 of the present chapter, we obtain the following assembly of volitives and volitions about future action:

imperatives	intentions/desires that someone *else* do x
intentives	intentions to do x
conatives	desires to do x.

Such a line-up of subjunctives of the will and volitions contrasts with this one:

optatives	idle wishes.

III

It is undeniable that evaluatives apt for expressing all-out present-tense summary evaluative thinking about action—like, indeed, all evaluatives—are indicatives, that is, sentences that have it as part of their meaning that their literal utterances characteristically are cases of saying that something is the case. Hare, as we have noted, acknowledges this. The syntax of illocutionary verbs like *assess* and *evaluate* points this way, we have seen: such verbs share the characteristic syntax of topic-focused representative illocutionary verbs like *describe* and *characterize*. And there is clear proof of this in the fact that evaluative illocutions performed in uttering evaluatives cannot be dissociated from representative illocutionary force. No one coherently can say things like: "*Autumn Sonata* is a good movie, but I'm not saying this is so", "I (you, he, etc.) ought to do *x*, but I'm not saying this is the case", and so forth. These sorts of remarks match the self-contradictoriness of comments like: "Snow is white, but I'm not saying it is", "Leave at once, but I'm not saying to you that you doing this", "I will leave at once, but I'm not committing myself to doing this", and so on. To the extent that evaluatives, and, in particular, evaluatives apt for expressing all-out present-tense summary evaluative thinking about action, are indicatives, the corresponding evaluative thinking is revealed as theoretical or cognitive. For, as we have seen, it is just such thinking, namely, belief, that indicatives are appropriate for putting into words. The point I wish now to develop is that indicatives are *all* that evaluatives like "I (you, he, etc.) ought to do *x*", and so on, are: that such evaluatives are not, in addition, sentences that incorporate some mood sign of the will. From this it follows that all-out present-tense summary evaluative thinking about action, one's own and others' (like, indeed, all evaluative thinking), is revealed, in the language of its expression, as *purely* cognitive or theoretical, and not, even in part, constituted by some volitional attitude.

I have already argued that evaluatives like "I (you, he, etc.) ought to do *x*", and so forth, do not include an imperative semantical component. Fundamentally, such evaluative illocutions as we characteristically directly perform in uttering *bona fide* examples of such evaluatives can be utterly divorced from directive illocutionary force. I now propose to argue that, similarly, evaluatives like "I (you, etc.) ought to do *x*", and so on, do not include an intentive or conative semantical component. Basically, such evaluative illocutions as we characteristically directly perform in uttering *bona fide* examples of such evaluatives can be completely detached from both commissive and conative illocutionary force. In addition, there is the overarching consideration that the imputation of intentive or conative meaning to evaluative terms as they occur in such evaluatives unacceptably multiplies the meanings of such terms, just as does crediting them in such cases with imperative meaning.

The issue, of course, is not whether evaluative illocutions performed in uttering such evaluatives ever are associated with directive, or commissive, or conative illocutions. They clearly *sometimes* are. Previously I gave examples of the association of evaluative and directive illocutions.[37] Similarly, evaluative and commissive, and evaluative and conative, illocutions can be associated. For example: I offer help to you by saying "I ought to help you"; or I express a desire to go to the beach by saying "It would be good to go to the beach". What I am insisting on is that this kind of phenomenon requires an interpretation that does not mistakenly impute moods of the will to the evaluatives involved. For such illocutionary associations, I contend, are not in any way *semantically* guaranteed: speakers perfectly well can dissociate their evaluative illocutions from *any or all* of the relevant illocutionary forces. To my mind, Searle's theory of indirect speech-acts affords the most plausible interpretation of what is going on when evaluative illocutions are accompanied by volitive illocutionary force. In such cases, on this picture, speakers indirectly perform volitive illocutions by way of making evaluative statements, or some such (ISA, Group 5, p. 66; Generalization 4, p. 72; Group 5, p. 80; Generalization 9, p. 82).

Semantically unexceptional remarks along the following lines show that evaluative illocutions performed in uttering evaluatives apt for expressing all-out present-tense summary evaluative thinking about action can be entirely detached from both commissive and conative illocutionary force:

(1) "You should leave immediately. I'm sure of that. But I want you to be clear that when I say this I'm not giving any commitment to act likewise in situations like this myself, or even, for that matter, expressing any inclination (desire) to so act in such circumstances. Nothing like that. I'm just letting you know what I'm sure you ought to do. But as I say: don't count on me to follow suit in like circumstances. I give no such undertaking. Indeed, I'm not even prepared to express an inclination (desire) so to act."

(2) "The right thing for me to do is to help her. I know that full well. But I'm not saying that I will, or, more generally, committing myself to helping anyone like her in similar circumstances. I remain silent on these matters, as I do on even whether I have any inclination (desire) to help her, or anyone like her similarly situated. All I'm prepared to tell you right now is what I know to be the right thing for me to do. For the rest: watch what I do."

And so forth. In such examples we have proof that evaluatives apt for expressing all-out present-tense summary evaluative thinking about action do not contain an intentive or conative semantical component. For, if they did, commissive or conative illocutionary force would be as inalienable from evaluative illocutions performed in uttering them as representative illocutionary force. But, as these examples illustrate, both commissive and conative illocutionary force are intelligibly dissociable from such evaluative illocutions.

Finally, there is the same general objection to the construal of evaluatives like "I (you, he, etc.) ought to do x" as (in part) intentives or conatives as applies to their construal as (in part) imperatives, namely, that such a construal unacceptably multiplies the meanings of evaluative terms. Briefly: evaluative terms cannot have intentive or conative meaning in sentences like

> You ought (subjunctive) to believe she is lying
> I ought (subjunctive) to feel ashamed

for the verbs they govern in such cases are not verbs of action.[38] Likewise, it is unintelligible that evaluative terms should have intentive or conative meaning in probability examples like

> Fred ought (indicative) to try to kill him tonight.

Yet there is good reason to think that such terms are univocal throughout categoricals like these and ones like

> I (you, he, etc.) ought (subjunctive) to do x

which employ verbs of action. For we can say things like

> You ought (subjunctive) both to believe she is lying and to do x
> It ought to be (indicative) that Fred will try to kill him tonight, and hence, (subjunctive) that I should do x

which depend for their generation on *ought* being univocal with respect to each of the conjuncts within its scope.[38]

To conclude. Evaluatives apt for expressing all-out present-tense summary evaluative thinking about action are only what they undeniably are, namely, indicatives. They do not include, in addition, a relevant volitive semantical component. Therefore, the evaluative thinking such evaluatives are suitable for expressing is revealed, in the language of its expression, as wholly cognitive or theoretical and nonvolitional. This has been my central argument in this chapter and the previous one.

If this argument is correct, we have an important result for the possibility of such weakness of will as concerns me. For, characteristically, there are two chief sources of concern about this possibility. First, there is the idea that there is a logically necessary relation between such evaluative thinking as characterizes the putative akrates, namely, full-fledged all-out present-tense summary evaluative thinking about his own action, and the presence in him of some corresponding volition to act. And, second, there is the idea that there is a logically necessary connection between having such a volition to act and intentionally acting in accordance with it. The result—that, as in the other-person case, all-out present-tense summary evaluative thinking about one's own action is wholly theoretical and nonvolitional—substantially undermines the initial source of worry about the possibility of weakness of will. For, to repeat what I said in Chapter 1, we can be assured, in this case, that such evaluative thinking as characterizes the putative weak-willed agent is never prevented from splitting off from some corresponding volition to act on his part by the way in which the inherently volitional nature of all-out present-tense summary evaluation about one's own action guarantees a logically necessary *because essential* relation between any full-fledged instance and having such a matching volition to act.

IV

A supplementary comment. Evaluative beliefs such as "I ought to do x" and "It is wrong to do x" constitute, respectively, attitudes of approval and disapproval. Such attitudes of approval and disapproval have often been construed as *feelings*—for example, by emotivists.[39] Prescriptivism, as developed by Hare, represents, I think, a considerable improvement over its immediate ancestor emotivism to the extent that it appreciates that affect or feeling is *inessential* to such attitudes of approval or disapproval.[40] Still, approval and disapproval *can* be feelings: feelings of approval and disapproval. It is, therefore, worth noting that this possibility can be accepted without in the least conceding that *volition* ever is, even in part, constitutive of such attitudes. For the simple fact is that cognitions, like volitions, can occur as feelings: just as there are volitional feelings, so there are cognitive or theoretical feelings.[41] For example, just as we can have feelings of desire, we can have feelings of suspicion; we can have felt expectations, as in presentiments ("I just feel that he will"); we can feel sure, confident, certain, convinced, and so on. Similarly, I suggest, feelings of approval and disapproval provide examples of *cognitive* feelings. Sometimes, indeed, such feelings assume the form of strongly felt convictions; feelings of moral approval and disapproval, for example, are often like this.

CHAPTER FOUR

Value and Reason

THE MOST FRUITFUL STRATEGY for establishing the possibility of weakness of will lies with a correct interpretation of all-out present-tense summary evaluative thinking about one's own action. That is the theme of this essay. Where there is a worry about whether weakness is possible, it characteristically stems from a view that there is a logically necessary connection between full-fledged instances of such evaluative thinking and certain volitional thinking on the part of the agent. The thesis I am developing is that all-out present-tense summary evaluation about one's own action is such as to allow the complete dissociation of any full-fledged instance of such evaluation from any accordant volition to act. So far what has been argued is that such evaluative thinking is totally theoretical or cognitive and nonvolitional; so it is out of the question for there to be any logically necessary *because essential or constitutive or intrinsic* relation between its full-fledged occurrences and the presence of corresponding volitions to act. But what of any suggestion to the effect that there is a logically necessary though *extrinsic* relation between full-fledged all-out present-tense summary evaluative thinking about one's own action and certain corresponding volitional thinking on one's part, at least where such evaluative thinking is (justificatorily) felicitous? By *felicitous* all-out summary evaluation, I mean all-out summary evaluation that is ultimately grounded in some consideration (or set of considerations) that *can* serve ultimately to justify it. This kind of suggestion, as I noted in Chapter 1, is reminiscent of classical writers like Plato and Aristotle, who assimilate all-out summary evaluation about action to prudential evaluation; and Mill, in rather similar vein, perhaps believed something like it.[1]

I think that the following is the most plausible interpretation of the present suggestion:[2] Full-fledged all-out present-tense summary evaluative thinking about one's own action, where felicitous, necessarily corresponds to certain (supporting) judgements wherein the existence of present value in one's acting a certain way, or reason for one so to act, is relativised to the satisfaction or achievement of certain anterior volitions or ends that one actually has; and such judgements as these (in Kantian terms, assertorial hypothetical imperative [ahi] evaluations) necessarily motivate one, in combination with the relevant antecedent volitions, to form some subsidiary consonant volition to act. The question before us in this chapter and the one to follow is what to make of the present suggestion under this interpretation.

In Chapter 1, I remarked that the second half of this suggestion so construed is itself problematic. For it is a difficult issue whether there is any such thing as logical necessitation of the will to secondary volition via anterior volition and relevant utilitarian evaluation. Even Kant, who is classically associated with a version of the thesis of logical necessitation, appears at times to allow for a breakdown in the transference of will from ends to (believed) necessary means.[3] But fortunately, as I also remarked earlier, this difficult issue is not one we need to settle here. For what in any case undercuts the proposal that there is a logically necessary *extrinsic* relation between full-fledged all-out present-tense summary evaluation about one's own action, where felicitous, and the presence of some matching volition to act is that it cannot be sustained that such evaluative thinking necessarily corresponds to certain ahi thinking. In sum, all-out present-tense summary evaluative thinking about one's own action can be felicitous and yet fail to be ultimately grounded in ahi thinking. This is what I shall argue in this chapter and in Chapter 5.

There are, in short, two generic facts about all-out present-tense summary evaluation about one's own action that are fundamental to the solution of the problem of how weakness of will is possible. That is what I am proposing in this essay. The first of these I argued for in Chapters 2 and 3, namely, that such evaluative thinking is wholly theoretical and nonvolitional. I argue for the second of these facts in this chapter and the one to follow—that such evaluation can, without infelicity, fail to be ultimately grounded in ahi thinking. The first generic fact tells against the view that there is a logically necessary *(because) intrinsic* connection between such evaluative thinking as characterizes the putative akrates and certain corresponding volitional thinking on his part. The second generic fact tells against the view that there is a logically necessary *extrinsic* relation between the two (at least where the evaluation is felicitous).

I

That all-out present-tense summary evaluative thinking about one's own action perfectly well can be felicitous and yet not be ultimately grounded in ahi judgements shows up in the relation between such evaluative thinking and corresponding judgements about present reason for oneself to act. Briefly: (1) such evaluative thinking is analysable in terms of such judgements, and (2), felicitous all-out summary judgements about present reason for oneself to act need not be ultimately grounded in ahi judgements. In this chapter my specific focus will be to establish (1); in Chapter 5 it will be to establish (2). To establish (1) I offer the following argument. The evaluatives apt for expressing all-out present-tense summary evaluation about one's own action are indicatives that characteristically contain primary or base evaluative terms like *good, right, ought,* and so on; and such evaluative terms, as applied to actions, are analysable in terms of the concept of reason. For the semantic common denominator of words like *good, right, ought,* and so on, is *of value;* and *x*'s being of value is tantamount to *x*'s being such that there is *something to be said for x;* which is *x*'s being such that there is *some reason for* x, where *x* is something upon which reasons coherently can be said to bear; and persons' actions are paradigm examples of things for which there can be reasons for and against.

II

What is basic in this argument is that *of value* is the semantic common denominator of evaluative terms like *good, right,* and *ought.* Consider, therefore, *good.* What does it mean to say, for example, that Bergman's *Autumn Sonata* is a good movie? I suggest that to say this is to make an *indefinite statement* to the effect that *Autumn Sonata* is a movie that possesses in great or high degree that characteristic, or set of characteristics, the having of which is the relevant standard of being of value (merit or worth): in brief, that *Autumn Sonata* is a movie *of great* or *high value (merit or worth).*[4]

It is important to stress that the varieties (and subvarieties) of goodness do not correspond to different meanings of the word *good.*[5] Consider hedonic examples like:

(1a)   good apple
(2a)   good time
(3a)   good company
(4a)   good smell
(5a)   good weather

understood as

(1b)   apple that is good in respect of being pleasant-tasting
(2b)   time that is good in respect of being fun
(3b)   company that is good in respect of being entertaining
(4b)   smell that is good in respect of being agreeable
(5b)   weather that is good in respect of being enjoyable.

(1a) understood as (1b) is equivalent to

(1c)   very pleasant-tasting apple.

(2a) understood as (2b) is equivalent to

(2c)   time that is a lot of fun.

(3a) understood as (3b) is equivalent to

(3c)   very entertaining company.

And so on.

What accounts for these equivalences, very clearly, is not that in (1a) *good* means *very pleasant-tasting,* whereas in (2a) it means *much fun,* and in (3a) *very entertaining,* and so forth, but rather that, in (1a) understood as (1b), *good in respect of being pleasant-tasting* means *very pleasant-tasting;* in (2a) understood as (2b) *good in respect of being fun* means *a lot of fun;* in (3a) understood as (3b) *good in respect of being entertaining* means *very entertaining,* and so on. Throughout (1a)–(5a) understood as (1b)–(5b), *good* retains one and the same *indeterminate* meaning, namely, *of great* or *high value (merit* or *worth).* What differ in determinate meaning are different adjectival expressions comprising *good* under differing adverbial modifications, namely, *good in respect of being pleasant-tasting, good in respect of being fun,* and so on. These differing adverbial modifications indicate the different hedonic qualities whose presences constitute the differing standards of being of value for the examples (1a)–(5a).[6]

These cases are instructive because it has been said, misguidedly, that *good* does not mean *pleasant* because it is an open question whether something pleasant is good. If there is anything here to the point, which is an open question, it is whether something that is *good so far as being pleasant goes* is also *good so far as concerns being moral;* but what this goes to show is that the former *whole phrase* does not mean the same as the latter *whole phrase. Good,* of course, does not mean *pleasant:* it means *of great* or *high value.* What means *pleasant,* or more accurately, *especially pleasant,* is the whole adjectival phrase *good in respect of pleasantness.* But of course it is not an open question whether what is good in respect of pleasantness—i.e., whether what is very pleasant—is good in respect of pleasantness—i.e., is very pleasant (cf. *VG,* ch. 4, p. 85).

Below are further illustrations that the varieties of goodness do not correspond to different meanings of the word *good.* Consider *prudential* and *altruistic* examples (cf. *VG,* ch. 3, pp. 41 ff) like:

(6b) good for me
(7b) good for the cat
(8b) good for the nation.

(6b)–(8b) are equivalent, in turn, to expressions like:

(6c) highly beneficial to me

(7c) in the great interest of the cat

(8c) to the great benefit of the nation.

In (6b)–(8b) *good* has one and the same indefinite meaning but occurs under modification from adverb-phrases of the form *for N*, i.e., in effect, *as far as concerns the condition of N*. What accounts for the equivalences between (6b) and (6c), (7b) and (7c), and (8b) and (8c), is that the whole expression *good relative to the condition of*, i.e., *of great* or *high value relative to the condition of*, means something like *very beneficial to*, or *in the great interest of*, or *to the great benefit of*.

Sometimes it looks as though *good* means *very useful* or *of great use*. For example, an expression like

(9b) good poison for killing cockroaches

is equivalent to one like

(9c) poison that is very useful (of great use) for killing cockroaches.

But appearances are deceptive in such cases of *utilitarian* goodness (again, cf. *VG*, ch. 3, pp. 41 ff). For what accounts for the replaceability of *good* in (9b) by *very useful* or *of great use* to yield the equivalent sentence (9c) is that being *good for a purpose* is being *very useful*, or *of great use*. It is noteworthy that prudential and altruistic goodness are subsumable under utilitarian goodness: being good for N, that is, in N's great interest, is a matter of being very useful for promoting N's well-being (cf. *VG*, ch. 3, pp. 42–43).

Instrumental and *technical* goodness fall into the by now familiar pattern (cf. *VG*, ch. 2, pp. 19 ff). Take instrumental examples like:

(10a) *K* is a good knife

(11a) *P* is a good pen.

Common definite counterparts for (10a) and (11a) would be

> (10c) *K* is a knife that is very smooth-cutting
> (11c) P is a pen that writes very legibly

respectively. This is given in part by the fact that *knife* and *pen* are functional nouns; that is to say, it is part of the meaning of *knife* that knives are instruments for cutting, and part of the meaning of *pen* that pens are instruments for writing.[7] The further specificity here derives from what are fairly typical "subjective settings"[8] of such essential purposes of knives and pens: agents commonly want to cut as smoothly as possible with knives and to write as legibly as possible with pens.

But (10c) and (11c) are not evidence that *good* sometimes means *very smooth-cutting* and sometimes *very legible-writing*. For (10c) and (11c) are got from (10a) and (11a) understood more fully as

> (10b) K is a knife that is good with respect to the degree of smoothness with which it cuts
> (11b) P is a pen that is good with respect to the degree of legibility with which it writes

respectively. In short: what means *very smooth-cutting* is not *good* but the whole adjectival expression *good with respect to the degree of smoothness with which such and such cuts,* and what means *very legible-writing* is not *good* but the whole adjectival expression *good with respect to the degree of legibility with which such and such writes.* Throughout *good* means simply *of great* or *high value (merit* or *worth).*

Closely allied examples of technical goodness tell a similar tale. Note:

> (12a) Quine is a good philosopher
> (13a) Nureyev is a good dancer
> (14a) George is a good administrator.

For (12a)–(14a) we might plausibly propose as determinate counterparts

(12c)   Quine is a very able philosopher
(13c)   Nureyev is a very skilful dancer
(14c)   George is a very efficient administrator

respectively.

But examples like these do not indicate that *good* can mean things such as: *very able, very skilful, very efficient, very competent, very adept, very proficient,* and so on. For sentences like (12c)–(14c) are got from sentences like (12a)–(14a) understood more fully as sentences like

(12b)   Quine is a philosopher who is good with respect to the degree of ableness with which he philosophizes
(13b)   Nureyev is a dancer who is good so far as concerns the degree of skilfulness with which he dances
(14b)   George is an administrator who is good in respect of the degree of efficiency with which he administers

respectively. In (12b)–(14b) goodness is relativised, in turn, to the ableness, skilfulness, and efficiency with which an agent exercises some ability, capacity, or skill. This indicates that what it is that means *being very able (very skilful, very efficient, etc.)* is not *being good* but *being good with respect to the degree of ableness (skilfulness, efficiency, etc.) with which so-and-so does something.*

Consider, finally, attributions of *supererogatory* goodness, such as occur in examples like

(15a)   It is good of Peter to help Paul

or its transform

(16a)   Peter is good to help Paul.

The difference between (15a) and (16a) is that in (15a) one calls Peter's deed good, whereas in (16a) one calls Peter good.[9] Now any of the following might serve as determinate correlates of (15a) and (16a) respectively:

$(15c_1)$–$(15c_4)$ It is very kind/very considerate/very thoughtful/very generous of Peter to help Paul

$(16c_1)$–$(16c_4)$ Peter is very kind/very considerate/very thoughtful/very generous to help Paul.

But, in such cases, $(15c_1)$–$(15c_4)$ and $(16c_1)$–$(16c_4)$ derive from (15a) and (16a) understood more fully as

$(15b_1)$–$(15b_4)$ It is good of Peter, as far as concerns kindness/considerateness/thoughtfulness/generosity, to help Paul

$(16b_1)$–$(16b_4)$ Peter is good, as far as concerns kindness/considerateness/thoughtfulness/generosity, to help Paul

respectively. So, where $(15c_1)$–$(15c_4)$ are determinate correlates of (15a), and $(16c_1)$–$(16c_4)$ are determinate correlates of (16a), we do not have evidence that *good* has various meanings. Throughout, *good* means *of great* or *high value (merit* or *worth);* but *good with respect to kindness* means something different from *good as far as concerns considerateness,* and so on. The lesson here is as elsewhere: the varieties of goodness are coordinate not with different meanings of the word *good* but with different meanings of adjectival expressions comprising *good* under differing adverbial modifications.

So far so good. I now want to attend to the evaluative term *right.* What does *right* mean? I suggest that to say something is right is to make an *indefinite statement* to the effect that the thing possesses in sufficient degree that characteristic, or set of characteristics, the having of which is the relevant criterion of being of value (merit or worth): in short, that it is *of sufficient value (merit* or *worth):* that it is *satisfactory* or *good enough.*[10]

The varieties of rightness do not correspond to various meanings of the word *right* any more than the varieties of goodness correspond to various meanings of the word *good.* With *right* it is exactly as it is with *good: right* does not have several meanings;

what differ in meaning are different adjectival phrases comprising *right* under different adverbial modifications. For example: the right thing for one to do for oneself (prudential rightness) is the action sufficiently beneficial to oneself; the right poison for killing cockroaches (utilitarian rightness) is the poison sufficiently useful for this purpose.[11] *K*'s being all right as a knife (instrumental rightness) might well be *K*'s being sufficiently smooth-cutting; *Z*'s being all right as a philosopher (technical rightness) might well be *Z*'s being sufficiently able; *x*'s being legally (all) right to do (legal rightness) is *x*'s being legally permissible to do; and so forth. But these examples do not bear witness to meanings of *right* such as: *sufficiently beneficial to, sufficiently useful, sufficiently smooth-cutting, sufficiently able, permissible,* and so on. For, in the prudential case, what means *sufficiently beneficial to* is not *right* but *right with respect to the condition of;* in the utilitarian case, what means *sufficiently useful* is not *right* but *right for a purpose;* in the instrumental case, what means *sufficiently smooth-cutting* is not *right* but *right as far as concerns the degree of smoothness with which such and such cuts;* in the technical case, what means *sufficiently able* is not *right* but *right with respect to the degree of ableness with which so-and-so does something;* in the legal case, what means *permissible* is not *right* but *right relative to a law;* and so on. Throughout, *right* has the one indefinite meaning: *of sufficient value (merit or worth): satisfactory* or *good enough.*

It is worth remarking at this point on the relation between the concept of *necessity* and the concept of *the right.* Sometimes saying that someone must, or is obliged to, or is required to, or is bound to, or has to, act, or choose to act, in a certain way, or believe something, or feel a certain way, or whatever, relative to some viewpoint, can be elucidated by saying that if the person does not act, or choose to act, in that way, or believe the thing in question, or feel the relevant way, he goes or does wrong, or makes a mistake, or is mistaken, relative to that viewpoint. For example: to say that *N* must do *x* in order to achieve his purpose of doing *y* can be explained by saying that *N* can fail to do *x* only on pain of making a mistake as far as concerns his achieving his purpose of doing *y;* saying that *N* is legally obliged, or morally bound, to do *x* can be explained by saying that, if *N* does not do *x*, he does wrong relative to the law or the moral point of view; *N*'s being rationally required to believe that *p* is something that can be elucidated by saying that, if N fails to believe p, he goes wrong in what he thinks so far as concerns being rational; and so on.

For such cases what seems to hold is this: the relevant modified necessity is analysable in terms of a corresponding modification of *the right*. So, for example,

(17)   N must do x in order to do y
(18)–(19) N is legally/morally obliged to do x
(20)   N is rationally required to believe that p

are to be analysed, respectively, as

(17)'   The right thing for N to do in order to do y is x
(18)'–(19)' The legally/morally right thing for N to do is x
(20)'   The rationally right thing for N to believe is that
         p.

The final evaluative term whose meaning I wish to consider is *ought*. The issue is what *ought* means in subjunctive- and indicative-governing instantiations of *ought to V*. I suggest that, whereas *good* and *right* mean, respectively, *of great* or *high value (merit* or *worth)* and *of sufficient value (merit* or *worth)*, *ought* means univocally, throughout its occurrences, *of most value (merit* or *worth)*: in a word, *best*.[12]

So, for example, to say subjunctively

(21)   I ought to leave at once rather than to remain
(22)   You ought to believe she is lying rather than that she is telling the truth
(23)   He ought to feel ashamed rather than pleased
(24)   There ought to be less suffering in the world than there presently is

is effectively to say, in turn,

(21)'   It would be better for me to leave at once than for me to remain

(22)′   You would do better to believe she is lying than to believe she is telling the truth

(23)′   It would be better for him to feel ashamed than for him to feel pleased

(24)′   It would be better for there to be less suffering in the world than there presently is.

Likewise, to claim indicatively

(25)   Fred ought to try to kill him tonight rather than tomorrow night

effectively amounts to claiming

(25)′   That Fred will try to kill him tonight is better than that Fred will try to kill him tomorrow night.

Just as there are varieties of goodness and modes of rightness, so there are varieties or modes of (to commit a barbarism) oughtness. For example, with respect to subjunctive-governing occurrences of *ought*, there is prudential oughtness ("I ought to leave at once so far as concerns me"), utilitarian oughtness ("I ought to spread this poison about to kill the cockroaches"),[13] moral oughtness ("He morally ought to feel ashamed"), rational oughtness ("You rationally ought to believe that she is lying"), and so on; and, with respect to indicative-governing occurrences of *ought*, there is just what we might call probabilistic oughtness ("In respect of being probable [or likely], it ought to be that Fred will try to kill him tonight").[14]

Familiar considerations apply at this juncture. To say that I ought to leave at once as far as concerns me is to say, in effect, that it would be in my greatest interest, or most beneficial to me, to leave at once; to say that I ought to spread this poison about in order to kill the cockroaches is effectively to say that spreading this poison about is what would be most useful on my part for killing the cockroaches; to say that, rationally, you ought to believe that she is lying is effectively to say that your believing she is lying is what is most rational; to say that, in respect of being probable, it ought to be that Fred will try to kill him tonight is to say, in effect, that Fred's trying to kill him tonight is what is most probable; and so on. But these equivalences are not witness to the several meanings of *ought*. For the semantic situation is this. In the prudential case, what means *in the greatest interest of*, or *most beneficial to*, is not *ought* but *ought* (understood as *best*) *as far as concerns the condition of*; in the utilitarian case, what means *most useful* is not *ought* but *ought* (understood as *best*) *for a purpose*; in the rational case, what means *most rational* is not *ought* but *ought* (understood as *best*) *as far as concerns being rational*; and in the probabilistic case, what means *most probable* is not *ought* but *ought* (understood as *best*) *in respect of being probable*.

Ought has had an unhappy life at the hands of philosophers. For example, A. C. Ewing contends that the action that ought to be done is the right action.[15] But this confuses what we ought to do with what we must do, or are obliged to do, or some such (cf. White, *MT*, ch. 10, pp. 157 ff). The concept expressed by *ought* is *weaker* than the concept of necessity; and this is something that can be explained in terms of the relation between *ought* and *best*, on the one hand, and certain modifications of necessity and corresponding modifications of *the right*, on the other. Thus, whereas to do other than what one morally ought to do is to act in a way that is *less than morally best*, to do other than what one morally must do, or is obliged to do, is to act in a way that, *from the moral perspective, falls short of being satisfactory*: that, *morally speaking, isn't good enough*.

In *Modal Thinking*, Alan White challenges the analysis of *being obliged* and *ought* in terms of what is best or what is right. In one place, he offers the argument:

> Obligation shares with its genus necessity—and with truth—the property called by logicians 'distribution through logical conjunction'. Thus, if I am obliged to give prizes to both *A* and *B*, then I am obliged to give a prize to *A* and obliged to give a prize to *B*. The notions expressed by 'best' and 'right' . . . do not have this property. It does not follow that because the best or right thing . . . is to give *A* and *B* a prize, therefore the best or right thing . . . is to give *A* a

prize and the best or right thing . . . is to give B a prize. Hence, we cannot give a correct analysis of *obligation* in terms of what is best or right (ch. 9, pp. 132–33).

In another place, White argues as follows:

It is the difference of what ought to be from either what is best or what is right that explains why 'It ought to be that p and q' implies and is implied by 'It ought to be that p and it ought to be that q'—since if p *and* q is owing, then p is owing and q is owing—whereas 'It is best (or right) that p and q' does not imply nor is implied by 'It is best (or right) that p and it is best (or right) that q'—since p and q cannot both be the best or the right thing (ch. 10, p. 143).

These arguments are hardly persuasive. For two things *can* both be the best or the right thing *relative to different sets of alternatives;* and *all* the examples in question, as examples of merely *logical* conjunction, are appropriately read as incorporating such relativisations. Thus, if I am obliged to give prizes to both A and B, then, as between giving and not giving A a prize, I am obliged to give A a prize, and, as between giving and not giving B a prize, I am obliged to give B a prize. And exactly likewise: if the best or the right thing is to give both A and B a prize, then, as between giving and not giving A a prize, the best or the right thing to do is to give A a prize, and, as between giving and not giving B a prize, the best or the right thing is to give B a prize. *Mutatis mutandis* for *ought* in comparison with *the best* or *the right.* If it ought to be that I should tell her and leave at once, then, as between telling and not telling her, I ought to tell her, and, as between leaving and not leaving at once, I ought to leave at once. Similarly: if the best or the right thing is that I should tell her and leave at once, then, as between telling and not telling her, the best or right thing is that I should tell her, and, as between leaving and not leaving at once, the best or the right thing is for me to leave at once.

Summing up: it is my contention that *of value* is the semantic common denominator of such primary or base evaluative terms as characteristically figure in evaluatives apt for expressing all-out present-tense summary evaluative thinking about one's own action. Paradigm examples of such terms which are grist to this mill are *good, right,* and *ought.* For these mean, respectively: *of great* or *high value, of sufficient value,* and *of most value.* It is important here not to be misled by the varieties or modes of goodness, rightness, and oughtness into thinking that the terms that correspond to these concepts have several meanings. This is not so. Throughout their occurrences, words like *good, right,* and *ought* have one and the same indefinite meaning. What differ in meaning are the expressions comprising these univocal evaluative terms (which express the possession of degrees of value) under different adverbial modifications.

III

It is the fact that *of value* is the semantic common denominator of such evaluative terms as characteristically occur in evaluatives apt for expressing all-out present-tense summary evaluative judgements about one's own action which fundamentally accounts for why such judgements are analysable as judgements about present reason for oneself to act. For to say that *value* attaches to something x is effectively to say that there is *something to be said* (or *adduced,* or *cited*) *for* (or *on the side of,* or *in favour of,* or *in support of*) x; and where x is something upon which reasons coherently can be said to bear—for example, desiring, wanting, intending, believing, having certain feelings, and *acting*[16]—this comes to saying that there is *some reason for x.*

So, for example, to issue all-out summary evaluations like

(26)   The thing it would be good for me to do is to leave at once

(27)   The right thing for me to do is to leave at once

(28)   I ought (subjunctive) to leave at once

is tantamount to saying, in turn,

(26)″   The thing there is much reason for me to do is to leave at once

(27)''   The thing there is sufficient reason for me to do is to leave at once

(28)''   There is most reason for me to leave at once[17]

given that (26)–(28), which involve ascriptions of value in varying degrees to actions, are respectively equivalent to

(26)'   The thing there is great value in my doing is leaving at once

(27)'   The thing there is sufficient value in my doing is leaving at once

(28)'   There is most value in my leaving at once.

These equivalences are comparable with those connected with sentences like:

(29)   The thing it would be good for me to desire is to leave at once

(30)   The right thing for me to believe is that she is lying

(31)   I ought to feel ashamed.

(29) involves the ascription of value to someone's desiring to do something, for which there can be reasons for and against, and is equivalent to

(29)'   The thing there is great value in my desiring is to leave at once.

In light of this, (29) is to be analysed as

(29)''   The thing there is much reason for me to desire is to leave at once.

(30) involves the ascription of value to someone's believing something, for which there can be reasons for and against, and is tantamount to

(30)'   The thing there is sufficient value in my believing is that she is lying.

In light of this, (30) analyses as

(30)″ The thing there is sufficient reason for me to believe is that she is lying.

Finally, (31) involves the ascription of value to someone's feeling ashamed, for which there can be reasons for and against, and is equivalent to

(31)′ It would be best for me to feel ashamed.

From this we see that (31) effectively comes to

(31)″ There is most reason for me to feel ashamed.

IV

To recap: the present overarching issue of concern is whether there is a logically necessary although *extrinsic* connection between full-fledged all-out present-tense summary evaluation about one's own action, at least where this is felicitous, and the presence of some matching volition to act. It seems that, for there to be such a connection, the evaluative thinking in question would have to correspond to certain ahi thinking. But such a picture cannot be sustained, I contend, because all-out present-tense summary evaluation about one's own action can perfectly well be felicitous and yet not be ultimately grounded in ahi thinking. The proof of this turns on the relation between such evaluative thinking and correlative all-out summary judgements about present reason for oneself to act. Such judgements as these can be felicitous without being ultimately grounded in ahi judgements; and all-out present-tense summary evaluative thinking about one's own action is analysable in terms of such judgements about reasons for acting.

The specific focus of the present chapter has been to establish this last point. The argument has been, in essence, that such primary or base evaluative terms as paradigmatically characterize such evaluatives as are apt for expressing all-out present-tense summary evaluation about one's own action are analysable in terms of the concept of reason because they express the possession of varying degrees of value, and the concept of something's being of value, as applied to actions, is analysable in terms of such an action's being such that there is some reason in its favour.

CHAPTER FIVE

Present Reason for Acting
and Prior Volition

IT REMAINS NOW to establish that felicitous all-out summary judgements about present reason for oneself to act need not be ultimately grounded in ahi judgements.

I

The moral point of view may well provide one way to approach this truth. For surely a judgement like

> (J1) There is morally more reason for me to do x than for me to do anything else

can serve as ultimate justification for another judgement like

> (J2) There is more reason for me to do x than for me to do anything else.[1]

Yet there is reason to doubt that judgements like (J1) about present moral reason for oneself to act, even where felicitous, are necessarily ahi judgements.

It is, however, highly debatable whether felicitous judgements about present moral reason for oneself to act do escape connection with ahi judgements. Philippa Foot, for example, seems to have argued[2] that, in the absence of good reason to think otherwise, felicitous judgements about present moral reason for action continue most plausibly to be identified, when fully spelled out, as

101

ahi's. Foot's overall position, however, is complicated by the fact that her focus is sometimes on whether moral reasons for action are desire-dependent (pp. 148-50), and sometimes—usually, in fact—on whether such reasons are dependent upon the agent's desire or interest[3] (which, she agrees, he need have no desire to promote; "Postscript", *VV*, p. 156).

Gilbert Harman's position is less equivocal. In *The Nature of Morality (NM)* Harman declares baldly that "Reasons derive from your desires, what you care about" (ch. 12, p. 148), and, in line with this general doctrine, that "Moral reasons . . . derive from an intrinsic concern or respect for others as well as yourself".[4] According to Harman, the intention to adhere to the principle of utility represents an important aspect of an intrinsic concern for others; so a central range of felicitous judgements about present moral reason for oneself to act are to be identified, explicitly, as ahi judgements wherein the existence of reason for oneself to act is relativised to one's anterior intention to adhere to the principle of utility (ch. 10, pp. 121 ff; chs. 12-13, pp. 137-62). For Harman, however, an intrinsic concern for the general welfare does not exhaust the other-regarding motivational source of present moral reason for acting; so not all felicitous judgements about present moral reason for oneself to act relate to one's intention to adhere to the principle of utility. But all such judgements about moral reasons, in Harman's view, are ahi's of one kind or another (ch. 13, pp. 160-62).

Neither Foot nor Harman, however, argues convincingly that felicitous judgements like (J1) are most plausibly construed as ahi judgements. Foot's position, as I have said, is not straightforward. Sometimes her argument seems to be that judgements like (J1) are, where felicitous, most plausibly construed as ahi judgements. But usually it seems to be the more general argument that such felicitous judgements are most plausibly read as hypothetical imperatives, assertorial (relativising reasons to agents' desires) or otherwise (relativising reasons merely to agents' interests). Moreover, in her discussion, Foot systematically fails to appreciate the relation between judgements like (J1) and corresponding judgements like "I morally should (ought to) do *x* rather than anything else", namely, that the latter are analysable in terms of the former.[5] For Foot thinks it is an open question whether, given that an agent morally should or ought to do something, there is a moral reason for him to do it[6]; and argues that, in the absence of proof to the contrary, it remains most plausible to think that whether there is such a moral reason for the agent to act depends upon his desires (or upon his desires or interests). In fact, however, to concede that an agent morally should or ought to do something is *ipso facto* to concede that there is a moral reason, indeed a strongest moral reason, for him to do it[7]; and to grant that it could be that an agent morally should or ought to do something regardless of his desires or of either his desires or interests is *ipso facto* to grant that an agent can have moral reason, indeed strongest moral reason, for doing something regardless of his desires or of either his desires or interests.

Unlike Foot, Harman is a friend of the "reasons" analysis of sentences like "I morally should (ought to) do *x*" (*NM*, ch. 10, pp. 115–24). But Harman's construal of felicitous judgements like (J1) as ahi judgements is unpersuasive because it is inspired by a mistaken view about reasons for action in general, namely, that all reasons for action are desire-dependent. For although self-interest, for example, provides us with reasons for acting, still (to anticipate a theme I develop later in this chapter), we do not necessarily have a concern for or interest in (promoting) our own interest (see Sec. 2 below). It is important not to confuse such diverse things as something's being *a* reason for *N* to act and some belief's being *N's* reason for acting. It is the *latter* which is conditional upon *N*'s having a suitably related anterior volition; for in such a state of affairs *N* acts the way he does because of his believing something (which he *takes* to be *a* reason[8] for him to act that way); and beliefs motivate to action only in combination with appropriate prior volitions.[9]

It seems to me that the critical issue for whether felicitous judgements about present moral reason for oneself to act are necessarily identical with ahi judgements is how we are to interpret the moral point of view. I do not propose to undertake here a philosophical analysis of the moral point of view. But it is to the present purpose to note the following. Among philosophers (and presumably others) it is a fairly common intuition that morality is fundamentally concerned, *in one way or another*, with what is good or bad for people (or perhaps, more generally, sentients). This intuition about the nature of the moral point of view has been well expressed by G. J. Warnock. In *Contemporary Moral Philosophy* (*CMP*, 1967), Warnock writes:

> . . . it appears at least enormously plausible to say that one who professes to be making a moral judgement *must* at least profess that what is in issue is the good or harm, well-being or otherwise, of human beings—that what he regards as morally wrong is somehow damaging, and what he regards as morally right is somehow beneficial. There is no doubt at all that, apart from its high degree of vagueness, this would not be a sufficient characterization of moral judgement; nevertheless it does appear to me to mention a feature which, in one way or another, any intelligible theory must recognise to be of central importance (ch. 5, sec. iii, pp. 57–58).

This is a theme Warnock returns to in his later piece *The Object of Morality* (*OM*, 1971). There he contends that morality is geared to "the amelioration of the human predicament" (ch. 2, p. 16). The idea, briefly, is this. The human situation is inherently such that things are prone to go badly for people. Prominent among the circumstances that constitute this situation as of this kind are the "limited sympathies" people have for one another. Morality is concerned with ameliorating the human predicament with respect to the potentially damaging effects of such limited sympathies (*OM*, ch. 2, pp. 17 ff). Warnock writes:

> There are two obvious ways in which, consequently, things in the human predicament are liable to go badly. For people are not simply confronted, whether as individuals or groups, with the problems of getting along satisfactorily in material conditions that may, in varying degrees, be ungenial or hostile. They are also highly vulnerable to other people; and they often need the help of other people. But, given 'limited sympathies', it cannot be assumed that

needed help will naturally be forthcoming; and it cannot even be assumed that active malevolence will *not* be forthcoming. And perhaps above all, there may be the impossibility of trust (p. 22).

He then goes on to suggest:

> . . . the 'general object' of morality . . . is to contribute to betterment—or non-deterioration—of the human predicament, primarily and essentially by seeking to counteract 'limited sympathies' and their potentially most damaging effects . . . its proper business is to expand our sympathies, or, better, to reduce the liability to damage inherent in their natural tendency to be narrowly restricted (p. 26).

The intuition that preoccupies Warnock is at the heart of various theories of the moral point of view. A notable example is simple utilitarianism, which posits the greatest happiness or well-being of the greatest number as the single topic of morality, and universal beneficence as the one basic moral virtue.[10] Another example is G. R. Grice's construal of the ground or foundation of (basic) morality in terms of the contractually harmonized interests of everyone.[11] Such *content-rich* interpretations of the moral point of view belong to what J. L. Mackie calls the *narrow* conception of morality. They contrast with purely *formal* interpretations like Hare's, which Mackie characterizes as belonging to the *broad* conception of morality. In *Ethics*, Mackie writes:

> A morality in the broad sense would be a general, all-inclusive theory of conduct: the morality to which someone subscribed would be whatever body of principles he allowed ultimately to guide or determine his choices of action. In the narrow sense, a morality is a system of a particular sort of constraints on conduct—ones whose central task is to protect the interests of persons other than the agent and which present themselves to an agent as checks on his natural inclinations or spontaneous tendencies to act. In this narrow sense, moral considerations would be considera-

tions from some limited range, and would not necessarily include everything that a man allowed to determine what he did (ch. 5, p. 106).

It is interesting, however, that even Hare, in spite of his broad, purely formal conception of morality, has drawn somewhat closer in his theorizing about morality to the intuition that the moral point of view is in some way geared to what is good or bad for people. In *Freedom and Reason,* Hare says:

> There is a sense of the word 'moral' (perhaps the most important one) in which it is characteristic of moral principles that they cannot be overriden . . . but only altered or qualified to admit of some exception. This characteristic of theirs is connected with the fact that moral principles are, in a way that needs elucidation, superior to or more authoritative than any other kind of principle. A man's moral principles, in this sense, are those which, in the end, he accepts to guide his life by, even if this involves breaches of subordinate principles such as those of aesthetics or etiquette (*FR* 9.3, pp. 168–69).

But in his more recent publication, *Moral Thinking (MrT,* 1981), Hare modifies this stance in a way that brings him nearer to the intuition in question.

Hare now contends that moral thinking has two levels: critical and intuitive (*MrT* 2.1, pp. 25 ff; 3.3, pp. 49 ff). Corresponding to these two levels are two kinds of moral principles: critical and prima facie. Critical principles are universal, highly specific prescriptive principles that an agent does not allow to be overridden. Prima facie principles, by contrast, are universal, relatively unspecific prescriptive principles selected by critical thinking, which an agent does allow to be overridden (*MrT* 2.3, pp. 31 ff; 3.5, pp. 53 ff). Hare comments:

> It will be noticed that such a more complex definition of 'moral' brings us somewhat nearer to the point of view of some (e.g., Warnock . . .) who think of themselves as my

opponents. They wish to insist that no purely formal definition of 'moral' can be given; it has to be defined either in
terms of possible contents of moral principles, or in terms of
possible reasons for or justifications of them. I am not for a
moment abandoning my formalist position; but in spite of it
(i.e., without making any other than formal moves) I have
allowed that a principle is being treated as moral (of the second subclass) if the justification for it, in the mind of the person who holds it, is of a certain sort. And when we have
worked out the implications of the method of critical thinking . . . we shall see that the justifications which it provides
will be of the same general sort as these writers are after. *For
well-conducted critical thought will justify the selection of prima
facie principles on the ground that the general acceptance of them
will lead to actions which do as much good, and as little harm, as
possible (MrT 3.8, pp. 61–62; my italics).*

The reason that well-conducted critical thought will justify the
selection of prima facie principles in this way is, according to
Hare, that critical decisions of principle, that is, choices of critical
principles (2.5, p. 40), will themselves be *act-utilitarian* decisions or
choices[12]; and at the level of critical thinking we will select as
general prima facie principles ones we calculate adherence to will
yield actions, and the like, most nearly approximating to those
which would be chosen if we were able to use critical thinking all
the time (*MrT* 2.6, p. 43; 3.3, pp. 49 ff).

The point I want to make for present purposes is this. The intuition with which even Hare's formal account of morality now
more nearly accords, namely, that morality is, in some way or
other, about what is good or bad for people, or perhaps, more
generally, sentients,[13] surely *is* extremely plausible. And this gives
us reason to doubt that felicitous judgements about present moral
reason for oneself to act are necessarily ahi judgements. For there
is a fairly obvious way in which the view in question can be ap-
pealed to in support of the claim that such judgements are not
necessarily identical with ahi judgements. Briefly, *however* the
moral point of view is correctly thought to take account of persons' (or sentients') interests—whether this be in terms of what is

in the greatest interest of the greatest number, or the contractually harmonized interests of everyone, or whatever—it will be purely *contingent*[14] whether an agent has the appropriate general concern for or interest in (promoting) such interests. Hence it will be false that anyone's felicitous judgement that he has moral reason to do something—understood as, in effect, the judgement that he has reason so to act relative to (the promotion of) the greatest well-being of the greatest number, or the contractually harmonized interests of everyone, or whatever—is necessarily an ahi judgement.

A final comment. It is debatable how central or basic *principles* (or *rules*) are to morality.[15] But this much is clear. A construal of morality in terms of principles need not support the view that felicitous judgements about present moral reason for oneself to act are ahi judgements. Something that does, of course, support that view is a construal of morality in terms of *persons'* principles, that is, principles to which persons subscribe, which they intend to follow. Hare and Harman represent this kind of interpretation of the moral point of view. But David A. J. Richards, in *A Theory of Reasons for Action*, for example, provides a sharp contrast. Richards, inspired by Kant (Richards, ch. 6, pp. 88–89) and Rawls (ibid., pp. 80 and 306 n. 11) writes:

> . . . the concept of morality and moral principles is equivalent to the concept of those ultimate standards of conduct which, if publicly known and generally acted on, perfectly rational egoistic men (consisting of all persons), from a position of equal liberty, and in the absence of any knowledge of their own *particular* desires, nature, and circumstances, but with knowledge of all other circumstances of human life and desire, would agree to as the standards to be used in regulating their actual relations to one another, whether in their common institutions or apart from them (ibid., p. 80)

As Richards acknowledges, it will be purely contingent whether anyone who judges that he has reason to act a certain way relative to (meeting the requirements of) one of these principles, that is, one of *the* principles of morality, has the relevant principle as one of *his* moral principles.[16] Insofar as such judgements about moral reason for action (which he accepts as analytically reductive of moral judgements containing terms like *ought* and *right*; see ch. 12, pp. 212 ff) enjoy a widespread "moving appeal to action", says Richards, the explanation must fundamentally be that

> . . . as a brute fact of human psychology, there is a widespread desire to be moral, and thus the information conveyed by certain propositions containing 'ought', 'under a moral obligation', 'it is the morally right thing to do', etc., has an intelligible relation to human desire, and thus to the human actions that those desires, in part, motivate (ch. 13, p. 242).

In a discussion entitled "The Natural Attitude of Morality", Richards tries to throw light on how it is that persons naturally come to desire to regulate their lives by the principles of morality (ch. 13, pp. 242 ff).[17]

To sum up: the issue before us is whether felicitous all-out summary judgements about present reason for oneself to act are of necessity ultimately grounded in ahi judgements. I think the answer to this is no; and it seems that morality may well provide one way to see this truth. For surely a judgement like (J1) about present moral reason for oneself to act can serve as ultimate justification for an all-out summary judgement like (J2) about present reason for oneself to act; yet there is reason to doubt that felicitous judgements like (J1) are necessarily identical with ahi judgements. For what seems critical here is the nature of the moral point of view to which such judgements about reason for action relativise the presence of reason; and it is very plausible to think that the moral point of view concerns, in some way or other, what is good or bad for people, or perhaps, more generally, sentients—which is something that need not, on any of its construals, interest an agent. Furthermore, some theorists propagate the idea that principles (or rules) constitute morality. This is a controversial claim, but it is worth noting that there are versions of this view—David Richards', for example—which do *not* support the contention that felicitous judgements about present moral reason for oneself to act like (J1) are necessarily ahi judgements. Such versions contrast with versions like Hare's or Harman's, which have it that morality is constituted by *persons'* principles.

II

In any case we need only appeal to judgements about present prudential or self-interested reason for oneself to act to see that felicitous judgements like (J2) need not be ultimately grounded in ahi judgements. For surely a judgement like

(J3) There is, so far as my own interest (good) is concerned, more reason for me to do *x* than anything else

can serve as ultimate justification for a judgement like (J2) (see fn. 1 above). Yet it is perfectly coherent that one should *not* have any concern for or interest in (promoting) one's own interest or good: that one should *not* have (the promotion of) one's own interest or good as an object of volition or end.

This last claim is debatable. Consider Kant's position, for example. Kant distinguishes between two kinds of hypothetical imperative: *problematical* and *assertorial*. The idea is that, by contrast with categorical imperatives, hypothetical imperatives say only that some action is "good for some purpose, *possible* or *actual*" (*FR*, p. 32).[18] Problematical hypotheticals concern possible purposes, assertorial hypotheticals actual purposes. According to Kant, hypothetical imperatives that are about our own happiness or well-being[19] are *assertorial*. For we necessarily have our own happiness or well-being as one of our ends. Kant writes:

> There is *one* end, however, which may be assumed to be actually such to all rational beings (so far as imperatives apply to them, viz., as dependent beings), and, therefore, one purpose which they not merely *may* have, but which we may with certainty assume that they all actually *have* by a

natural necessity, and this is *happiness*. The hypothetical imperative which expresses the practical necessity of an action as means to the advancement of happiness is *assertorial*. We are not to present it as necessary for an uncertain and merely possible purpose, but for a purpose which we may presuppose with certainty and *a priori* in every man, because it belongs to his being (*FR*, p. 33).

Kant appears in this passage to be claiming, in effect, that it is analytic of beings like us—that it is part of the concept of a human being—that such beings have a concern for or interest in (promoting) their own interest or good: that such beings have (the promotion of) their own interest or good as an object of volition, as an end. But this is surely mistaken. There is nothing in the least incoherent about our not having a concern for or interest in (promoting) our own interest or good. For, just as we can be indifferent or hostile toward (the promotion of) the good or interest of another, so we can be indifferent or hostile toward (the promotion of) our own interest or good.

Consider the altruistic case. Certain feelings or moods, or, more generally, frames or sets of mind, can (and indeed, all too familiarly do) render us indifferent to promoting the good of another. This is a theme Michael Stocker has exploited in his paper ''Desiring the Bad: An Essay in Moral Philosophy''.[20] With respect to the desire to benefit others, Stocker writes:

> Lack of this desire is commonplace. Through spiritual or physical tiredness, through accidie, through weakness of body, through illness, through general apathy, through despair, through inability to concentrate, through a feeling of uselessness or futility, and so on, one may feel less and less motivated to seek what is good. One's lessened desire need not signal, much less be the product of, the fact that, or one's belief that, there is less good to be obtained or produced, as in the case of a universal Weltschmertz. Indeed, a frequent added defect of being in such ''depressions'' is that one sees all the good to be won or saved and one lacks the will, interest, desire, or strength (p. 744).

Similarly, certain moods, or frames or sets of mind, can (and indeed, all too commonly do) make us hostile toward another, desiring not to benefit, but to harm, the other. In this connection Stocker writes:

> Just as helping another can be the direct and proper object of desires and appetites, so can harming others . . . One way to see this is that in certain loving or caring moods, helping is precisely what is desired. So too, in other moods, harming is precisely what is desired. When we feel furious, hurt, envious, jealous, threatened, frustrated, abandoned, endangered, rejected, and so on, what we often seek is precisely the harm or destruction of someone, and not always the "offending party" (p. 748).[21]

Good examples are the way to convince that such psychologies are possible for us. Take the case of Monique, in Simone de Beauvoir's *The Woman Destroyed*.[22] Monique's story unfolds by means of diary entries. For Friday 17 September Monique makes this entry:

> Here I am with still another protégée on my hands. When I left Colette after dinner on Wednesday it was so mild that I drove down to the Latin quarter: I sat on the terrace of a café, and I smoked a cigarette. At the next table there was a teen-age girl who gazed longingly at my packet of Chesterfields: she asked me for one. I talked to her; she evaded my questions and got up to go. She was about fifteen, neither a student nor a prostitute and she aroused my curiosity—I suggested giving her a lift home in my car. She refused, hesitated, and then in the end confessed that she did not know where she was going to sleep. She had escaped that morning from the Centre where the Public Assistance had put her. I kept her here for two days. Her mother, who is more or less mentally deficient, and her step-father, who loathes her, had given up their rights over her. The judge who is in charge of her case promised to send her to a Home where she will be taught a trade. Meanwhile for these six

months she has been living 'provisionally' at this Centre. . . I promised her I should move heaven and earth to get her transferred to a Home and she let herself be persuaded to go back to the Centre. I boiled with anger when I saw her go through the door, her feet dragging, her head bowed. She is a pretty girl, not stupid at all, very sweet-tempered, and all she asks is to work—her youth is being hacked to pieces: hers and the youth of thousands like her. Tomorrow I shall ring up Judge Barron (pp. 107–8).

But by Thursday 16 December there is this contrasting entry:

Marguerite has run away again and they can't find her. She went off with a girl who is a real tramp. She will go on the streets, steal things. It is heartbreaking. Yet my heart is not broken. Nothing touches me any more (p. 186).

Monique's earlier concern for Marguerite is characteristic of her as she then is (pp. 108–9). But not only does Monique change and become indifferent to Marguerite's fate, there are others she becomes hostile to and wants to hurt. Maurice, her husband, for example. For Saturday 27 November she concludes:

I irritate him a little more every day. I don't mean to. And yet there is a part of me that does. When he seems too cheerful and unconcerned I say to myself, 'This is too easy'. And then any excuse is good enough for me to destroy his peace of mind (p. 159).

Then there is her ill will toward Noëllie Guérard. For Friday 17 December Monique makes the entry:

I saw them again yesterday evening. I was prowling about L'An 2000, where they often go. They got out of Noëllie's convertible; he took her arm; they were laughing. At home, even when he is being pleasant, he has a grim expression: his smiles are forced. 'It's not an easy position . . .' When he is with me he never forgets it for a moment. With her, he

does. He laughed, unconstrained, careless, easy. I felt like
doing her an injury. I know that is female and unfair; she
has no duty towards me—but there it is (p. 187).

De Beauvoir portrays Monique's metamorphosis as wrought
by her emotional reaction to learning that Maurice is having an af-
fair with Noëllie. Monique's life has been built around her relationship with Maurice. But toward the end of September she
records: "Maurice has changed. He has let himself be eaten by his
profession" (p. 110). The drift apart angers her, and she struggles
to control herself (p. 112). But then Maurice tells her the devas-
tating truth: he has been deceiving her; there is another woman
in his life, Noëllie Guérard (pp. 112 ff). Monique is stunned,
then angry and "choked with bitterness" (pp. 114–115). But
she becomes self-critical—"I have never made proper allowance
for untruth" (p. 116); and in this mood, and encouraged by a
friend, Isabelle, she decides on a policy of patience—"It is I who
would be unnatural—childish, really—if I were not to accept this"
(pp. 116–17). Indeed, she even reassures herself that things are
not so bad as they seem—"I don't have to get him back: I have
never lost him" (p. 117).

But there is to be no reprieve for Monique. She continues to
try for self-control, but at times her anger breaks through, and she
and Maurice have heated interchanges (pp. 121 ff). She is
obsessed by painful images of intimacies between Maurice and
Noëllie—"They are in their pyjamas; they are drinking coffee,
smiling at one another . . . there is an image that hurts me"
(p. 122). She oscillates between doubting the soundness of her
policy of forbearance to wondering whether she should be "still
more understanding, more detached, more full of smiles"
(pp. 128 ff). Maurice and Noëllie go away for a weekend, and
Monique, left alone, becomes distracted by jealousy—"I had
thought I could preserve myself from jealousy; not at all"
(pp. 130 ff). She becomes distracted to the point of exhaustion and
disorientation—"I am tired of asking myself questions and not
knowing the answers. I am out of my depth. I no longer recognise
the flat" (p. 132).

Eventually she decides it is time to act. She asks Maurice to let them spend a weekend together in Nancy—"I should like him to rediscover a happiness and a closeness that he has rather tended to forget—rediscover it with me; and I should like him to remember our past, too" (p. 138). Maurice tries to avoid the weekend, but Monique is determined—"I broke out in rebellion; for the first time I cried in front of him" (p. 139). Maurice arranges things, and they go away. But before they do Monique visits Marguerite. Her concern for Marguerite is still well and truly alive (p. 139).

The weekend proves a disaster. Come Saturday evening Maurice rejects Monique's sexual advances. Monique becomes desperate to understand this development (pp. 141 ff). Gradually a new fear begins to insinuate itself into her thinking—"Could it conceivably be that Maurice *does* prefer [Noëllie] to me?" (p. 146). More than ever she feels the need to be reassured about her physical attractiveness to men. She contacts an admirer, Quillan. This has a mixed result. It is clear that Quillan is still keen on her; but where does that get me? she asks herself: "It has not made me any more desirable to myself" (p. 146). She becomes progressively stupefied by her doubts and unhappiness (p. 148). Until very recently she has felt humiliated by what people have been thinking and saying about her and Maurice (pp. 143–44). But she is beyond that now—"I'm beyond caring what people think. I am too utterly destroyed" (p. 149). Things concentrate into this for her: "It's a matter of survival" (p. 149). She becomes obsessed with how much time Maurice is spending with Noëllie and starts to spy on him (pp. 150 ff). This leads to further scenes with Maurice (p. 152).

In the midst of all this Monique still manages time out for Marguerite, and for her daughter Colette, who has been ill. But for Saturday 20 November there is just the abrupt entry:

> Saw Marguerite. Spent a good deal of time with Colette. But nothing worth recording (p. 153).

For the most part Monique's energies are directed toward self-control. *But she is filled with anxiety and bitterness. Sometimes she loses the struggle with herself, and strikes out at Maurice.* For Saturday 27

November she makes the diary entry about Maurice noted above, in the preliminary to this précis (pp. 158–59).

The crisis now deepens. In a hideous scene, Maurice lets loose at her: she had not hesitated to make him give up a resident post; she was jealous of his work; she was a "castrating woman"; a possessive, overbearing, and encroaching mother and wife; and he, for his part, has not loved her for years and has been going to bed with other women for as long (pp. 160–62). Monique is left distraught—"I asked him to go away. I stayed there, shattered, trying to grasp this scene, trying to disentangle the true from the false" (p. 163). Later Maurice retracts some of the things he said (pp. 164–65). But Monique is haunted by "pitiless memories": cues in the past that all was not well between Maurice and her but which she had preferred to ignore (pp. 163, 166–67). She is filled with confusion about them both—"all at once I no longer recognise us, neither him nor me" (p. 167). Her mood is one of disillusionment with her life—"The whole of my past life has collapsed behind me"; and she is left enervated (p. 168).

Her birthday comes. On that day she has a talk with Maurice "full of trust and friendliness, quite detached—as if it were not a question of ourselves at all" (p. 178). She briefly deceives herself—"I ended up by believing Noëllie did not exist . . . Illusions: sleight of hand" (p. 180). But the deception is short-lived—"In fact this comfortable talk has not changed anything in the very least" (p. 181). The mood of inertia and disillusionment persists—"Maurice's love gave every moment of my life meaning. Now it is hollow. Everything is hollow—things are empty: time is empty. And so am I" (p. 183). Self-criticism sets in—"I had an inspiration this morning: the whole thing is my fault. My worst mistake has been not grasping that *time goes by*" (p. 183). Her past life becomes for her "a riddle, a source of bitter distress" (p. 185). She wonders, with fear, to what extent she has not been a good mother. There are painful memories to suggest that this is what Maurice really thinks, as he blurted out earlier, but later denied—"If I have failed with the bringing up of my daughters, my whole life has been a mere failure. I cannot believe it. But soon as doubt so much as touches me, how my mind reels!" (p. 186). Monique is exhausted—"What exhausts me is the way he is kind one day and surly and unaffectionate the next" (p. 186). She is close to utter despair—"Should I settle down definitely into despair?" (p. 186). But as yet she resists this—"'But then he would quite forget what I was once and why he had loved me" (p. 186).

It is at this point in her dark night of the soul that Monique receives news that Marguerite has run away again and makes the entry for Thursday 16 December that is quoted in the prelude to this précis. What we see here is this. *Having run the gamut of her feelings and poised on the verge of utter despair, Monique is too tired and self-preoccupied to care anymore what happens to Marguerite.* Her next diary entry, for Friday 17 December, I also listed in the preliminary to this précis. In this case, the vision of Noëllie with Maurice arouses in Monique, who has suffered so much because of her loss of Maurice to Noëllie, bitterness and jealousy; and *bitter and jealous, Monique wants to injure Noëllie.*

So much for indifference and hostility toward the good of another. In sum: such psychologies, in which we fail to have a concern for or interest in (promoting) the good of another, are possible for us because of the ways certain feelings or moods, or, more generally, frames or sets of mind, can affect us. Fine-grained characterizations of nights of the soul like de Beauvoir's characterization of Monique's, which are perfectly coherent and, indeed, all too true to our tribe, bear compelling witness to this.

For present purposes what is especially important is this. Just as, in certain moods or frames of mind, we can be indifferent or hostile toward another and, hence, not have any concern for or interest in (promoting) the good or interest of the other, so too, we can, in certain moods or frames of mind, be indifferent or hostile toward ourselves and, hence, not have (the promotion of) our own interest or good as an end. Stocker draws attention to this in his paper "Desiring the Bad" (pp. 744–45, 748).

That self-indifference is as possible a psychology for us as indifference to another is also attested to by de Beauvoir's characterization of how Monique is affected by the "maladies of the spirit". For, in quite coherent fashion, de Beauvoir depicts Monique as progressively ceasing to care what happens to *herself* as well as to Marguerite. The morning of her birthday, Monday 13 December, Monique makes the following entry into her diary:

The hideous fall into the abyss of sadness. From the very fact of being sad one no longer has the least wish to do anything cheerful. Now I never put on a record when I wake up. I never listen to music any more, never go to the cinema, never buy myself anything pleasant. I got up when I heard Mme Dormoy come in. I drank my tea and ate a piece of toast to please her. And I look forward over this day, still another day that I must get through (p. 177).

From this point on, the motif of Monique's listlessness and loss of interest in herself gradually assumes prominence.

On the evening of Sunday 19 December Maurice suggests to her that she and he spend Christmas Eve and New Year's Eve together. She hears this with "a sudden spurt of happy surprise" (p. 188). But the experience proves depressing for her. From time to time she can believe in their relationship again; but such trust quickly dissipates (p. 189). Early in January she learns the shocking truth. Over Christmas and New Year she has been "acting as the stop-gap": Noëllie has been away (p. 191). She is choked with rage and goes for Maurice furiously (p. 192). Later, her mood is one of "heavy inertness" and doom. Maurice is leaving for a holiday with Noëllie, and she expects that on his return he will end things between them (p. 192). Left alone, she becomes more and more indifferent to herself, and lets herself go very badly (pp. 192–93).

Her daughter Colette finds her in a pitiful condition and takes her home. Something Maurice says when he returns revives her hope. He wonders out loud whether he really loves Noëllie (pp. 197–98). But such hope is false hope, and Monique soon suffers disappointment. Maurice spends more evenings with her for a while; but he and Noëllie have had a falling out and, with their reconciliation, he gives most of his time to Noëllie again (pp. 198–202). Monique is shattered—"I am losing all grip on things. I am falling lower, lower all the time" (p. 203). She complains of her lack of energy to look after herself—"What useless energy you need for even the simplest things when all liking for life is gone!" (p. 205); she writes of her relentless suffering and of how welcome an easy death would be—"I go on bleeding. If only my life could run out of me without my having to make the slightest effort!'' pp. 205); she talks of her crippling loss of her sense of herself—''There was once a man who lost his shadow. I forget what happened to him, but it was dreadful. As for me, I've lost my own image'' (pp. 207–8); she writes of how trapped she feels—''Go mad. That would be a good way out . . . It is a way out that is closed to me'' (p. 208); she expresses her disgust with her own body—''I stand in front of the looking-glass: how ugly I am! How unlovely my body is!'' (p. 209).

Monique has been haemorrhaging (p. 209). She has been to see a psychiatrist—''I was sent to the psychiatrist, I was made to recover a little strength before the final blow was struck'' (p. 210). Maurice announces he is going to find a place for himself. She is devastated—''I said no, I screamed, I insulted him'' (p. 210). The psychiatrist encourages her to accept Maurice's move, at least for a while. She does this—''The psychiatrist has put the last touches to my demoralization. I no longer attempt to struggle'' (p. 211). *She is now ''without any anger, totally reduced, empty''* (p. 211). Toward the end of her diary entry for 8 March she writes:

> . . . what I do know is that in a year or two, when I have got used to it, he will live with Noëllie. Where shall I be? In my grave? In an asylum? I don't care. I don't care about anything at all (pp. 212–13).

Her self-indifference is complete.

Maurice and others press her to go and spend a fortnight in New York with another daughter Lucienne—''Lucienne would take delivery of me at the other end—a parcel that is trundled about, an invalid, or a halfwit'' (p. 213). In New York she tries to get from Lucienne some understanding of herself and what has happened with Maurice. But this too proves hopeless. She does not like what she sees of Lucienne's way of life—''work, going out, brief encounters'' (p. 217). She detects in Lucienne a ''refusal to love'' and blames herself for this—''My sentimentality sickened her and she has warped herself in trying not to be like me'' (p. 217).

Monique is now in all respects the woman destroyed. She thinks of herself as a dead woman—"A dead woman who still has years to drag out"; and her energy is drained to the point of immobility (p. 219). She has no will to live—"Do not stir: ever. Stop the flow of time and of life" (p. 220). But she knows that there is to be no reprieve: she will live, and she is utterly alone. She is very afraid (p. 220).

De Beauvoir's coherent fine-grained portrait of Monique's psychological undoing bears compelling witness to the fact that self-indifference is a possible psychology for us because of how we can be susceptible to certain moods or frames of mind. There are, of course, many coherent, and, indeed, authentic[23] examples of such susceptibility in literature.[24]

So much for having no concern for or interest in (promoting) one's own interest or good as a matter of self-indifference. It is also possible not to have such a concern or interest as a matter of self-hostility. For, just as we can, in certain moods or frames of mind, be hostile toward another, desiring not to benefit but to harm the other, so too, we can, in certain moods or frames of mind, be hostile toward ourselves, desiring not to benefit but to harm ourselves. *We can, for example, desire our own harm rather than good, out of contempt or disgust for or hatred of ourselves, out of self-directed anger, guilt, or shame, and so on* (cf. Stocker, p. 748).

I am reminded of André Gide's universal misanthrope, Strouvilhou, in *The Counterfeiters*. Strouvilhou declares to another character, Passavant: "in so far as I am a man, I despise and hate myself as much as I do my neighbours" (p. 305). Earlier, he and Passavant have had the following conversation:

" . . . Philanthropy was never one of my strong points".

"I know, I know", said Passavant.

"Nor egoism either. That's what you don't know. . . . People want to make us believe that man's single escape from egoism is a still more disgusting altruism! As for me, I maintain that if there's anything more contemptible and more abject than a man, it's a lot of men. No reasoning will ever persuade me that the addition of a number of sordid units can result in an enchanting total. I never happen to get into a tram or a train without hoping that a good old accident will reduce the whole pack of living garbage to a pulp; yes, good Lord! and myself into the bargain. I never enter a theatre without praying that the chandelier may come crashing down, or that a bomb may go off; and even if I had to be blown up too, I'd only be too glad to bring it along in my coat pocket—if I weren't reserving myself for something better. You were saying?. . ." (p. 304).

Then, too, there is Lafcadio Wluiki in Gide's *The Vatican Cellars.* There we read:

> As soon as Julius had turned the corner of the passage, Lafcadio pushed to the door and bolted it. He ran to the drawer, pulled out the pocket-book, opened it at the last tell-tale page, and, just at the place where he had left off several months before, he wrote in pencil in a large hand, sloping defiantly backwards and very unlike the former:
>
> For having let Olibrius poke his dirty nose in this book . . . . 1 punta
>
> He took a penknife out of his pocket; its blade had been sharpened away until nothing was left of it but a sharp point like a stiletto, which he passed over the flame of a match and then thrust through his trouser pocket, straight into his thigh. In spite of himself he made a grimace. But he was still not satisfied. Leaning upon the table, without sitting down, he again wrote just below the last sentence:
>
> And for having shown him that I know it . . . 2 punte
>
> This time he hesitated, unfastened his trousers, and turned them down on one side. He looked at his thigh in which the little wound he had just made was bleeding; he examined the scars of similar wounds, which were like vaccination marks all round. Then, having once more passed the blade over the flame of a match, he very quickly and twice in succession plunged it into his flesh . . .
>
> His anger had cooled a little, when . . . (pp. 53–54).

In his anger with himself, Lafcadio desires *precisely* (cf., fn. 21 above) to injure himself as a self-punishment; and, as the reference to ''the scars of similar wounds'' indicates, it is often like this with Lafcadio.

Such psychologies of self-hostility, engendered by such frames of mind as self-contempt or hate, self-directed anger, and so on, seem perfectly possible, and, indeed, authentic pathologies.

To sum up: the overarching thesis of this section has been that we need only appeal to judgements about present prudential or self-interested reason for oneself to act to appreciate that felicitous all-out summary judgements like (J2) about present reason for oneself to act are not necessarily ultimately grounded in ahi judgements. The argument, in essence, has been this: a prudential or egoistic judgement like (J3) surely can serve as ultimate justification for a judgement like (J2); yet, *pace* Kant, it is perfectly coherent that one should *not* have a concern for or interest in (promoting) one's own interest or good; for, just as, as a result of certain moods or frames of mind, we can be indifferent or hostile toward another and, hence, not have (the promotion of) the good or interest of that other as an object of volition, so too, as a result of certain moods or frames of mind, we can be indifferent or hostile toward ourselves and, hence, not have (the promotion of) our own interest or good as an end. That self-indifference and self-hostility are in these ways possible psychologies for us, as indifference and hostility toward others are in similar ways possible psychologies for us, is attested to by the evident coherence of relevant examples. Such examples, indeed, are not merely coherent, they are authentic, in that they capture how it actually or really could be (and in certain cases all too commonly is) for people like us.

III

The project for this chapter has been to establish that felicitous all-out summary judgements about present reason for oneself to act need not be ultimately grounded in ahi judgements. I have argued that morality may well provide, and that prudence certainly does provide, a way to see this truth. The moral point of view may well provide a way to see this truth, because a moral judgement like (J1) surely can serve as ultimate justification for a judgement like (J2); yet there is reason to doubt that felicitous cases of the former are ahi judgements. Principally: it is plausible to think that morality takes for its topic, in some way or other, the interests of people (or perhaps, of sentients); and it will be purely contingent whether an agent has the appropriate general concern for or interest in (the promotion of) such interests. Prudence, for its part, certainly provides a way to see the truth in question. For prudential judgements like (J3) surely can also serve as ultimate justifications for judgements like (J2); yet, *pace* Kant, it is logically or conceptually open for one, *qua* human being, *not* to have a concern for or interest in (promoting) one's own interest or good. Just as indifference and hostility toward others are possible psychologies for us, so too, and in analogous ways, are self-indifference and self-hostility. The necessity of ever-present self-love, as much as the necessity of ever-present love of others, is a chimera.

This completes my argument that there is no logically necessary although *extrinsic* relation between full-fledged all-out present-tense summary evaluation about one's own action, where such evaluation is felicitous, and the presence of some corresponding volition to act. As I have said before, it seems that, for there to be such a relation, the evaluative thinking in question will have to correspond to certain ahi thinking. But such a correspondence cannot be sustained because all-out present-tense summary evaluation about one's own action perfectly well can be felicitous and yet not ultimately grounded in ahi thinking. The proof of this turns on the connection between such evaluative thinking and the corresponding all-out summary judgements about present reason for oneself to act. Such judgements can be felicitous without being ultimately grounded in ahi judgements; and all-out present-tense summary evaluative thinking about one's own action is analysable in terms of such judgements about reasons for acting. In Chapter 4, I argued the latter point. In this chapter I have argued the former.

CHAPTER SIX

Conclusion

I began this essay with the question: Is it possible for an agent to be weak-willed in what he does? By which I meant: Can an agent knowingly and intentionally act against his full-fledged all-out summary better judgement, or judgement about what is right, or some such, when he is free to act in accordance with it, has the relevant know-how, and has present to mind the judgement that now is the time to act? I commented that, although, pre-reflectively, such weakness of will would seem a familiar, every-day phenomenon, the possibility of such a phenomenon has seemed problematic to some philosophers, ancient and contemporary. For, on their view, typically, such all-out summary evaluation about action as characterizes the putative weak-willed or akratic agent is connected with the presence in him of certain volitional thinking, and this thinking, in turn, is connected with action, in ways that conflict with the possibility of weakness of will so understood.

I have argued that no *such* problem about the *logical* or *conceptual* possiblity of weakness arises. The way to see this, I maintain, is through a correct interpretation of all-out present-tense summary evaluative thinking about one's own action. For such evaluation about action as characterizes the putative akrates is full-fledged thinking of this kind; and such thinking is such as to allow the complete dissociation of any full-fledged (felicitous) instance from any corresponding volition to act. In the first place, all-out present-tense summary evaluative thinking about one's own action is wholly theoretical and nonvolitional. This rules out any logically necessary (*because*) *intrinsic* relation between such evaluative thinking as characterizes the putative akrates and certain matching volitional thinking on his part. In the second place,

124

all-out present-tense summary evaluative thinking about one's own action can, without infelicity, fail to be ultimately grounded in ahi thinking. This rules out any logically necessary *extrinsic* connection between such evaluative thinking as typifies the putative akrates (at least where this is felicitous) and certain accordant volitional thinking on his part.

Briefly, there is no logical problem about the possibility of weakness of will of the kind canvassed because it is perfectly *coherent* for us to be *unintegrated* in a certain way, namely, not to have any volitions to act that correspond to our (felicitous) all-out present-tense summary evaluations about our own actions.

Notes

CHAPTER ONE: The Possibility of Weakness of Will

1. By, for example, an agent's all-out summary better judgement I mean an unconditional better judgement, or judgement about what is simply better, on his part, made on the basis of what he takes to be all the available relevant considerations. I borrow the term *all-out* from Donald Davidson. See his paper "Intending" in his *Essays on Actions and Events* (hereafter, *EAE*), pp. 96 ff.

2. *Paradise Lost,* in David Masson (ed.), *The Poetical Works of John Milton* II; Bk 9, lines 738 ff (Eve); lines 997 ff (Adam).

Compare Thomas Aquinas, *Summa Theologiae (S.Th.),* Q163, article 4.

3. The extent to and way in which Plato is committed to construing the good in terms of pleasure is problematic. See I. M. Crombie, *An Examination of Plato's Doctrines,* I, *Plato on Man and Society,* ch. 6, pp. 225 ff; Paul Shorey, "Plato's Ethics", in Gregory Vlastos (ed.), *Plato,* II, pp. 24 ff.

4. See Gerasimos Santas, "The Socratic Paradoxes", *Philosophical Review* 73 (1964): 147–64; and "Plato's *Protagoras* and Explanations of Weakness" in Geoffrey Mortimore (ed.), *Weakness of Will,* pp. 37–62.

5. Plato's primary focus is on putative akratic action as action that contravenes an agent's evaluative *knowledge*. But sometimes he conducts his discussion in terms of belief, e.g., *Protagoras,* 358c–d. Compare *Meno* 97b: "Therefore true opinion is as good a guide as knowledge for the purpose of acting rightly." Aristotle, for his part, declares the distinction between knowledge and belief to be of no consequence for whether akrasia is possible: *Nicomachean Ethics,* 1146b24.

6. See Terry Penner, "Thought and Desire in Plato" in Vlastos (ed.), *Plato,* II, pp. 96–118; Gary Watson, "Skepticism about Weakness of Will", *Philosophical Review* 86 (1977): 319–21.

7. Compare G. E. M. Anscombe, "Thought and Action in Aristotle", in Renford Bambrough (ed.), *New Essays on Plato and Aristotle*, pp. 151 ff.

8. See W. P. R Hardie, "Aristotle on Moral Weakness" in Mortimore (ed.), *Weakness of Will*, pp. 69–94; David Wiggins, "Weakness of Will, Commensurability, and The Objects of Deliberation and Desire," *Proceedings of the Aristotelian Society* 79 (1978–79): 258 ff. Of special interest is Anthony Kenny's paper "The Practical Syllogism and Incontinence" in his *The Anatomy of the Soul*, pp. 28–50. Here Kenny takes issue with Aristotle's alleged socratism about akrasia. In the case of the so-called weak akrates, he argues, Aristotle provides for an agent's "acting in a way which he fully knows at the time to be wrong". Central to his argument is the view that Aristotle's Fourth Solution (*Nicomachean Ethics*, 1147a–b) involves not two syllogisms, one of reason and one of desire, but a single syllogism with two premises, one universal (something like "Taste nothing pleasant") and a composite minor premise ("Everything sweet is pleasant and this is sweet"). In ch. 14 of *Aristotle's Theory of the Will*, however, Kenny modifies his stance. He persists with the interpretation that weak akrasia involves a single syllogism (pp. 158–59) but now accepts the view that in such a case "the conclusion, though drawn, is only half-had as a piece of knowledge" (pp. 163n, 155–66).

9. Compare Davidson, "How Is Weakness of the Will Possible?" in his *EAE*, pp. 21–22, 29–30.

10. Compare Aquinas, *S. Th.*, Q.155.

11. Donleavy, *The Saddest Summer of Samuel S.*, pp. 76 ff.

12. *Paradise Lost* Bk 1, lines 159 ff.

13. Jean Genet, *The Thief's Journal*, pp. 202–3; and *Funeral Rites*, pp. 72–73, 157–58, 198.

14. See Hardie, "Aristotle on Moral Weakness, pp. 70–71. Aquinas follows Aristotle in this distinction: *S.Th.*, Q155, article 2.

15. Compare Aquinas, *S. Th.*, Q156, article 4.

16. See Anscombe, "Thought and Action", pp. 143 ff, esp. 146–47; Kenny, *Will, Freedom and Power*, pp. 16–18; and *Aristotle's Theory of the Will*, pp. 69 ff.

17. See Santas, "The Socratic Paradoxes", pp. 162–63; Anscombe, "Thought and Action", p. 156; Amelie Rorty, "Plato and Aristotle on Belief, Habit and *Akrasia*", *American Philosophical Quarterly* 7 (1970): 50.

18. Hare concentrates on all-out summary evaluation about action

identified as moral evaluation, and, accordingly, on weakness of will conceived as moral weakness.

19. See Hare, *FR* 5.2, pp. 69–70; compare Plato, *Protagoras,* 358d.

20. For Hare on "proper universal" imperatives, see *LM* 11.5, 12.4–5.

21. In *LM* Hare actually speaks of second-person commands addressed to ourselves. But in his self-quote in *FR* he omits this qualification.

22. See *FR* 5, passim, especially pp. 82–84.

23. In *FR* Hare interprets having a volition to act in terms of the illocution—assenting to a first-person singular imperative, and more generally, desiring (willing) that someone should do something in terms of the illocution—assenting to an imperative (*FR* 3.2, p. 34; 5.4, pp. 71–73). Elsewhere ["Wanting: Some Pitfalls" (hereafter, "Wanting") in Robert Binkley, Richard Bronaugh, and Ausonio Marras (eds.), *Agent, Action and Reason,* pp. 81 ff, esp. 91 ff], Hare defends against certain objections Kenny's suggestion in *Action, Emotion and Will* that desires or intentions to act are sayings-in-the-heart of first-person singular commands. This obscure suggestion at least more evidently respects the difference between thought and speech.

24. For a recent expansion of this theme see Hare, *Moral Thinking,* 3.7, pp. 58 ff.

25. Compare Watson, "Skepticism About Weakness of Will", pp. 321–23; Robert Audi, "Weakness of Will and Practical Judgement", *Noûs* 13 (1979): 182 ff, 188–89.

26. In *Philosophical Papers,* ed. J. O. Urmson and G. J. Warnock, p. 198. Of course, succumbing to temptation connotes giving in to the flesh, and, as I previously remarked, putative weakness does not necessarily involve such desires. Compare Davidson, "How Is Weakness of the Will Possible?" in *EAE,* p. 29.

27. Compare *S.Th.,* Q155, article 3, and Q156, article 1, p. 23. For a contrasting discussion, see Watson on weakness and compulsion, "Skepticism about Weakness of Will", pp. 323 ff.

28. Davidson returns to the theme of incontinence in his more recent paper "Paradoxes of Irrationality," in Richard Wollheim and James Hopkins (eds.), *Philosophical Essays on Freud,* ch. 17, pp. 289–305. There Davidson argues that any satisfactory explanantion of irrational phenomena like incontinence will contain some of the most important features (broadly conceived) of Freud's attempts to explain irrationality. These theses are: (1) that the mind is partitioned into a number of semi-

autonomous parts, (2) that such subdivisions of the mind have a structure similar to that needed to explain ordinary intentional actions, and (3) that certain mental events can be mere causes of some other mental events in the same mind (pp. 289–91, 303–4). In the case of incontinence, Davidson argues, this can be seen in the following way. The akrates, insofar as he acts irrationally, is properly credited with the second-order principle: I ought to do what I judge to be best, all things considered. Otherwise "pure internal inconsistency" does not enter the picture (pp. 296–97). "A purely formal description of what is irrational in an akratic act", writes Davidson, "is, then, that the agent goes against his own second-order principle that he ought to act on what he holds to be best, everything considered" (p. 297). (This characterization of the akrates as inconsistent inasmuch as he is irrational is one of the most notable developments in Davidson's thinking about incontinence. Contrast "How Is Weakness of the Will Possible?", *EAE*, pp. 40–41.) Such irrationality, according to Davidson, is satisfactorily explained in just this way: there is a mental cause that is not a reason for what it causes. Specifically, the akrates, in doing what he does, ignores his second-order principle, and for this he has a reason, that is to say, a reason for ignoring the principle, but what he does not have is a reason against the principle, that is to say, a reason against acting on his own best judgement (pp. 296–99).

The explanation of incontinence in these terms accords with Freud's third thesis. But now, says Davidson, there is this problem: How can one mental event cause another mental event without being a reason for it? To meet this problem, Davidson claims, it seems we must assume that the mind is divided into internally consistent or rational quasi-independent structures (pp. 299–301). Such parts of the mind are defined in terms of function: "The breakdown of reason-relations defines the boundary of a subdivision" (p. 304). For incontinence the picture that emerges is this: we are to suppose "two semi-autonomous departments of the mind, one that finds a certain course of action to be, all things considered, best, and another that prompts another course of action. On each side, the side of sober judgement and the side of incontinent intent and action, there is a supporting structure of reasons, of interlocking beliefs, expectations, assumptions, attitudes and desires" (p. 300). In this way, says Davidson, we see that a satisfactory explanation of irrationality accords, in addition, with Freud's first and second theses (pp. 303–4).

Having canvassed certain difficulties with this favoured account of irrationality (pp. 301–3), Davidson notes, in conclusion, that the presence of a mental cause of something for which it is not a reason is a necessary but not sufficient condition of irrationality (p. 305).

For another discussion of the relevance of Freudian theory to the explanation of irrational phenomena like incontinence, see David Pears' paper "Motivated Irrationality, Freudian Theory and Cognitive Dissonance" also in Wollheim and Hopkins (eds.), *Philosophical Essays*, ch. 16, pp. 264–88.

29.   Compare Audi, 'Weakness of Will and Practical Judgement", pp. 192–93.

30.   See Audi, pp. 181 ff.

31.   See Audi, p. 194; and Michael Bratman, "Practical Reasoning and Weakness of Will", *Noûs* 13 (1979): 160–61.

32.   Davidson, "Intending", *EAE*, pp. 96–102.

33.   But compare his remarks in "How Is Weakness of the Will Possible?", *EAE*, pp. 26–27.

34.   See John R. Searle, "Indirect Speech Acts" in Peter Cole and Jerry L. Morgan (eds.), *Syntax and Semantics: Speech Acts* 3, pp. 59–82.

35.   Searle's classificatory term for the kind of illocutionary force with which imperatives are semantically associated. See Searle, "A Classification of Illocutionary Acts", *Language in Society* 5 (1976): 11.

36.   Searle's classificatory term for the kind of illocutionary force with which indicatives are semantically associated. See Searle, pp. 10–11. I have recently noticed, however, that Searle now prefers to talk of *assertive* rather than representative illocutionary force. See the reprint of Searle's article in his *Expression and Meaning*, ch. 1, pp. 1–29; also his "Introduction", p. viii, fn. 1.

37.   Compare Hare, "Wanting", pp. 89–90; Anscombe, *Intention*, sec. 36, pp. 67–68.

38.   See Searle (on Austin) on commissives, "A Classification of Illocutionary Acts", pp. 11–12.

39.   And certain other putative phenomena naturally so described. See Audi, "Weakness of Will and Practical Judgment", pp. 181 ff.

40.   See Anscombe, *Intention*, sec. 36, pp. 67–90; William P. Alston, "Wants, Actions, and Causal Explanation", in H.-N. Castañeda (ed.), *Intentionality, Minds and Perception*, pp. 320 ff; Audi, "The Concept of Wanting", *Philosophical Studies* 24 (1973): 1–21; Richard Brandt and Jaegwon Kim, "Wants as Explanations of Action", *Journal of Philosophy* 60 (1963): 425–35; Paul M. Churchland, "The Logical Character of Action-explanations", *Philosophical Review* 79 (1970): 214–36; Davidson, (a) "How Is Weakness of the Will Possible?" *EAE*, pp. 23–24; (b) "Freedom to Act", *EAE*, pp. 76 ff; Stuart Hampshire, *Freedom of the Individual*, p. 36; Pears,

"Sketch for a Causal Theory of Wanting and Doing" in his *Questions in the Philosophy of Mind*, pp. 108 ff; Charles Taylor, *The Explanation of Behaviour*, pp. 26–53; Raimo Tuomela, "Explanation and Understanding of Behaviour", in Juha Manninen and Tuomela (eds.), *Essays on Explanation and Understanding*, pp. 194 ff; Georg Henrik von Wright, (a) "Practical Inference", *Philosophical Review* 72 (1963): 165 ff; (b) *The Varieties of Goodness*, pp. 168–71; (c) "On So-called Practical Inference", *Acta Sociologica* 15 (1972): 39–53; (d) *Explanation and Understanding*, pp. 96 ff; (e) "Replies" in Manninen and Tuomela, pp. 371 ff.

41. See Davidson, "How Is Weakness of the Will Possible?", *EAE*, p. 26.

42. Such logical necessitation seems implausible in the case of anterior volitions that are merely desires. See Jaegwon Kim, "Intention and Practical Inference", in Manninen and Tuomela, pp. 254–55; and von Wright, "Replies", also in Manninen and Tuomela, pp. 395–96. Contrast von Wright, "Practical Inference", pp. 165–66 and 169–71.

43. For a discussion of some related difficulties, see Kim, "Intention and Practical Inference", pp. 254 ff; and von Wright, "Replies", pp. 399–400.

44. Kant's parenthesis in the first quote frequently has gone unheeded. For example, Alan Donagan cites this passage in support of the claim: "I take it to be analytic that if a man unconditionally intends to bring about a certain end *E*, and judges that his doing *A* is required for bringing about *E*, he must intend to do A" ["Alternative Historical Explanations and Their Verification", *Monist* 53 (1969): 76]. Compare von Wright in "On So-called Practical Inference", p. 45. Roy Edgley, by contrast, draws attention to the parenthesis: *Reason in Theory and Practice*, 4.11, pp. 137–47, esp. 140 ff. See too M. J. Scott-Taggart, "Comment: 'Kant, Conduct and Consistency' " in Stephan Korner (ed.), *Practical Reason*, pp. 226–27, 249–50, fn. 37. H. -N. Castañeda is sensitive to the presence of the parenthesis in the first quote and to its absence in the second: *Thinking and Doing*, ch. 11, sec. 5, pp. 300–303. For Kant, indeed, it would seem that it is the *universal* possibility of a breach between actual motivation and judgements of practical reason that explains the *imperativity* of the language of practical reason (*FP*, pp. 30–31, 66, 72). At once phenomena and noumena (*FP*, pp. 67 ff), we are not holy wills (*FP*, pp. 11, 31, 54, 56).

45. Von Wright's characteristic focus has been on the necessitation of the will *to action* through cognition and volition. Sometimes, however, his focus has been specifically on the transference of volition from a primary

to a secondary volition. For example: "Practical Inference", pp. 169–71; "On so-called Practical Inference", pp. 44–45, 47–48. But note "Replies", p. 399.

46. See "Practical Inference", pp. 165–66, 169–71; *The Varieties of Goodness*, ch. 8, sec. 7, pp. 167–71.

47. See *Explanation and Understanding*, ch. 3, pp. 96 ff, esp. 116–17; "Replies", pp. 399, 421–25.

48. Compare Michael Stocker, "Desiring the Bad: An Essay in Moral Psychology", *Journal of Philosophy* 76 (1979): 744–45, 748.

49. See Kim, "Intention and Practical Inference", pp. 255–56; von Wright, "Replies", p. 399; Brian O'Shaughnessy, *The Will*, 2, pp. 304, 308–9, 320.

50. See Aristotle, *Nicomachean Ethics*, Bk 6, 1139b; Hume, *A Treatise of Human Nature*, Bk 5, Part 3, sec. 3. Compare Davidson, "Actions, Reasons and Causes", *EAE*, pp. 3 ff, O'Shaughnessy, p. 52.

51. See, for example, Hampshire, *Thought and Action*, pp. 166–68; Don Locke, "Reasons, Wants and Causes", *American Philosophical Quarterly* 11 (1974): 169–79. Contrast Davidson, "Actions, Reasons and Causes", *EAE*, p. 11; Kenny, *Will, Freedom and Power*, pp. 116–19.

52. See W. H. Walsh, "Kant's Concept of Practical Reason" in Korner (ed.), *Practical Reason*, pp. 191–94. Compare Hare, *LM* 3.2, pp. 36–37.

53. See Thomas Nagel, *The Possibility of Altruism*, p. 11.

54. Compare Korner, *Kant*, pp. 162–63; Walsh, "Kant's Concept" pp. 207 ff.

55. See William K. Frankena, "Obligation and Motivation in Recent Moral Philosophy", in A. I. Melden (ed.), *Essays in Moral Philosophy*, pp. 40 ff; Nagel, *The Possibility of Altruism*, ch. 2, pp. 7 ff.

56. Compare Gilbert Harman, *The Nature of Morality*, ch. 6, pp. 70 ff.

57. The argument here, briefly, is as follows. Every prima facie reason can be formulated as a predicate R and characterized as a reason by a formula of the form: For all persons p and events A, if R is true of A, then p has prima facie reason to promote A. Such a predicate R provides prima facie reasons primarily for things to which it applies, and derivatively for things that promote that to which it applies primarily (ch. 7, pp. 47 ff). There are certain formal or structural conditions on any system of prima facie reasons for action which derive from basic features of our human makeup and which constitute that system as a motivational structure that makes possible pure prudence and pure altruism (chs. 3 & 4, pp. 13–23;

ch. 14, pp. 143–46). In the prudential case the relevant condition is *timelessness*. In the case of altruism it is *objectivity*. The condition of tense-or timelessness ensures that the influence of primary reasons is transmitted over time and, thereby, entails a prudential (ch. 6, pp. 36–37) constraint on practical reasons (ch. 6, pp. 45–56; ch. 7, pp. 47–49, 54–56; ch. 8, pp. 61 ff). The condition of objectivity on practical reasons allows the derivative influence of primary reasons to be transmitted across persons (ch. 10, p. 93). Objectivity amounts to the requirement on any practical reason that there *not* be within its defining predicate R any free occurrence of the agent-variable p. For example: (p,A), (If $(\exists q)$ (A will prolong q's life), then p has prima facie reason to promote A). Objective reasons are reasons for the *occurrence* of the things of which they hold true, reasons for *anyone* to want and promote those things to which they apply. Subjective reasons, by contrast, within whose defining predicates the agent-variable p occurs freely, are reasons for *particular individuals* to want and promote those things to which they apply. For example: (p,A) (If A will prolong p's life, then p has prima facie reason to promote A) (ch 10, pp. 90 ff). There is a requirement on any system of reasons for action that subjective reasons be submitted to a procedure of objectification to yield corresponding objective reasons (ch. 10, p. 90). Objectivity entails an altruistic requirement on practical reasons, given a certain substantive theory of primary subjective values or reasons, namely, that such value attaches to what is in one's *own* interest (ch. 8, pp. 74–76; ch. 9, p. 89; ch. 10, pp. 97–98; for complications, see ch. 13, pp. 126 ff).

Such formal conditions as timelessness and objectivity on any system of prima facie reasons for action admit interpretation in terms of a metaphysics of the person (ch 3, p. 14). Timelessness is the practical expression of that fundamental conception of ourselves as temporally persistent beings, equally real over time, which we, as humans, in a certain sense, necessarily possess, at least to some degree (chs. 3 & 4, pp. 13–23; ch. 8, pp. 58 ff). Objectivity is the practical expression of that basic conception which we, as humans, in a certain sense, necessarily have of ourselves, at least to some degree, as single persons among others equally real. For objective reasons are the *sine quibus non* of our retaining intact in our practical reasoning that dual conception of ourselves as ''I'' and as ''someone'' which is critical to this self-conception. Only objective reasons allow us to make impersonal judgements about reasons for action *to the same effect*, and, in particular, to the same *motivational* effect, as corresponding personal judgements about reasons for ourselves to act (chs. 3 & 4, pp. 13–23; chs. 11 & 12, pp. 99–124). Failure to acknowledge timeless reasons indicates a certain breach in the relevant conception of oneself, namely, one's *practical* dissociation from oneself as a temporally extended individual (chs. 3 & 4, pp. 13–23; ch. 8, pp. 58 ff). Failure to accept reasons for action as ultimately objective represents a similar breakdown in one's identification with oneself as just one person among others fully real, namely, *practical* solipsism (ch. 11, pp. 107 ff; ch. 12, pp. 116 ff). Such areas of selective dissociation are possible, but the acknowledgement of timeless and objective reasons is, even so, relatively inescapable for us, given how deep-seated as features of our human makeup are the relevant senses of ourselves (ch. 1, pp. 3–6; chs. 3 & 4, pp. 13–23; ch. 12, p. 124; ch. 14, pp. 143–46).

58. See Stephen Darwall, "Nagel's Argument for Altruism", *Philosophical Studies* 25 (1974): 125–30; Marilyn Reba, "A Second Look at Nagel's Argument for Altruism", *Philosophical Studies* 25 (1974): 429–34; G. F. Scheuler, "Nagel on the Rationality of Prudence", *Philosophical Studies* 29 (1976): 69–73; Nicholas L. Sturgeon, "Altruism, Solipsism, and the Objectivity of Reasons", *Philosophical Review* 83 (1974): 374–402.

CHAPTER TWO: Evaluatives, Imperatives,
and Evaluative Thinking

1. See also Hare, "Descriptivism" in W. D. Hudson (ed.), *The Is-Ought Question*, pp. 240–58.

2. Paper 5 in his *Practical Inferences*, pp. 74–93.

3. *Words and Deeds: Problems in the Theory of Speech Acts*, ch. 3 ff.

4. See G. J. Warnock, "Hare on Meaning and Speech Acts", *Philosophical Review* 80 (1971): 83–84. Compare Hare, "Appendix: Reply to Mr. G. J. Warnock", in *Practical Inferences*, p. 98.

5. Holdcroft, *Words and Deeds*, ch. 3, pp. 43–44; ch. 6, p. 101. See Holdcroft's argument against Searle's construal of the syntactic forms associated with mood as *general* illocutionary-force indicators: ch. 3, pp. 33 ff; ch. 4, pp. 46 ff, esp. pp. 53 ff. Compare J. R. Searle, "Austin on Locutionary and Illocutionary Acts", *Philosophical Review* 77 (1968): 405–24.

6. Ch. 11, pp. 220–21. See too Kenny, *Will, Freedom and Power* (1975), ch. 3, pp. 38–39. Compare G. E. M. Anscombe, *Intention*, sec. 32, pp. 56–57.

Holdcroft himself (ch. 6, p. 97) refers to Kenny's article "Practical Inference", *Analysis* 26 (1966): 65–75, where Kenny makes the same point. Compare Searle, "A Classification of Illocutionary Acts" (hereafter CIA) *Language in Society* 5 (1976): 3–4.

7. For a critical review of Holdcroft, see D. Cooper, *Mind* 89 (1980): 146–149.

8. In the terminology I adopt, commissives (see Chapter 1 above, fn. 38) are the *illocutions* with which the intentive-mood sign is semantically associated, as directives (see Chapter 1, fn. 35) are the illocutions with which the imperative-mood sign is semantically associated, and representatives (see Chapter 1, fn. 36) the illocutions with which the indicative-mood sign is semantically associated.

9. Compare Searle, "Austin on Locutionary and Illocutionary Acts", pp. 405–25; and Hare, "Austin's Distinction between Locutionary and Illocutionary Acts", in *Practical Inferences,* pp. 100–14, esp. pp. 110 ff. See the discussion of Searle in Holdcroft, *Words and Deeds,* chs. 3–4 (n.b. fn. 5 above). Holdcroft's pessimism about attempts to characterize mood meaning in terms of generic illocutionary-force potential is unpersuasive. He writes:

> But how, one might ask, is the very general illocutionary force potential 'built into' the meaning of an imperative related to the specific illocutionary acts that can be performed by uttering it? Searle seems to think that the relation is like that between genus and species, so that in the case in question 'tell (one to)' is the generic verb, and 'order', 'insist', 'request', etc., the specific ones. However, 'tell (one to)' is plainly insufficiently general to qualify as the generic verb. Maybe, to order someone to do something is to tell him to do it. But to dare him to do it is not to tell him to do it, any more than to request him to do so is to tell him to do so. Moreover, it is difficult to see what suggestion would fare better.
>
> It is difficult too to see how there could be a genus/species relationship of the sort Searle envisages for indicatives, i.e., such that,
>
> (a) The potentiality for performing the generic act is possessed by a sentence in virtue of the fact that it is of a certain grammatical type, namely, an indicative: and,
>
> (b) All other illocutionary acts performable by literally uttering a sentence of that type involve performing the generic act.
>
> Perhaps the most plausible candidate would be asserting. But though, for instance, hinting may involve asserting, it is not a specific way of asserting, what is hinted is not asserted, and neither is what is suggested. Estimating is not asserting (ch. 3, pp. 39–40; cf. ch. 4, pp. 53–54).

Holdcroft is undoubtedly right that, in the imperative case, *tell (one to)* "is plainly insufficiently general to qualify as the generic verb". Searle, like Hare (e.g., p. 111), is wrong in thinking differently. Likewise, Holdcroft is surely correct that, in the indicative case, *assert* "is plainly insufficiently general to qualify as the generic verb". Even so, it seems perfectly possible, *pace* Holdcroft, to characterize mood meaning in terms of generic illocutionary-force potential. For we can rely on specifications like the following: literal utterances of indicatives characteristically are cases of saying that something is the case; literal utterances of imperatives characteristically are cases of saying or putting it to hearers that they (should) act in certain ways; literal utterances of intentives characteristically are cases of committing oneself to act in certain ways; and so on.

10.   Compare Searle, "Meaning and Speech Acts" in C. D. Rollins (ed.) *Knowledge and Experience*, pp. 28–37. And the ensuing debate: Zeno Vendler, "Comments", pp. 38–42; Paul Benacerraf, "Comments", pp. 43–49; Searle, "Rejoinders", pp. 50–54.

11.   P. T. Geach, "Ascriptivism", *Philosophical Review* 69 (1960): 223; "Assertion", *Philosophical Review* 74 (1965): 461 ff. Compare David Zimmerman, "Force and Sense", *Mind* 89 (1980): 214–33.

12.   At least with respect to the application of this condition to syntactical transformations of prescriptivism's favoured categorical affirmatives, e.g., "This is a good *x*". But see sec. 5 of the present chapter.

13.   Compare Warnock's final remark in "Hare on Meaning and Speech Acts", p. 84: "The central objection, I would think, to Hare's doctrine about 'good' is not that, if its meaning were explained 'in terms of' some speech act, one could not then accommodate the obvious fact that the word means the same in conditionals and so forth as in simple indicative sentences. The central issue is the simpler one, whether there is any reason to think that the meaning of the *word* in fact *should* be explained 'in terms of' any speech act". Hare's response to this paper appears as "Appendix: Reply to Mr. G. J. Warnock" in *Practical Inferences*, pp. 94–99.

14.   The symbolism fairly well speaks for itself. 'N' represents nouns and pronouns. 'V' represents verbs. $N_i = N_i$; $N_i \neq N_j$; and so on. 'V + ' represents verbs followed by whatever objects they have (compare Zeno Vendler, *Adjectives and Nominalizations* [*A & N*] ch. 3, p. 35, fn. 1). 'Subj' abbreviates 'subjunctive'.

15.   See Vendler, *A & N*, ch. 2, pp. 30–31; ch. 4, pp. 56, 61–63; *Res Cogitans (RC)*, ch. 2, pp. 20–21, 24; Searle, CIA, p. 17. In the subjunctive matrix, the *should* of *shall* can occur in a subjunctive-equivalent construction. See Vendler, *A & N*, ch. 4, fn. 1, p. 56; and A. R. White, *Modal Thinking*, ch. 10, fns. 1 and 2, p. 162.

16.   Illocutionary point or purpose, which provides a good basis for

constructing a taxonomy of illocutions (see Searle, CIA, pp. 10 ff), corresponds to what Searle in *Speech Acts* calls the *essential conditions* on illocutions (see Searle, *SA* 3.1, pp. 60, 66–67; CIA, p. 3).

17. Contrast Searle, CIA, pp. 2, 11. According to Searle, the characteristic illocutionary point of directives is to try to get addressees to act in certain ways. See my comment, ch. 3 below, end of sec. 1.

18. CIA, pp. 12–13. Compare Austin's *behabitives* in *How to Do Things with Words*, lecture 12, p. 159.

19. See Vendler, *RC*, ch. 3, pp. 31–32, 35.

20. Compare Searle's "Comment" under the analysis of thanking: *SA* 3.4, p. 67.

21. It is of interest that I can commend or praise you for something you have done or are presently engaged in doing but not for something you have yet to do, so that my expressing my approval of your doing *x* tomorrow *cannot* be a case of my commending or praising you for that future action.

22. In his 1957 paper "Geach: Good and Evil", Hare writes: "It may be that Geach has not noticed the difference between commending and recommending"; and continues in a footnote: "We normally use 'recommend' when a *particular* choice is in question but 'commend' when a thing is being mentioned as in general 'worthy of acceptance or approval' " [Philippa Foot (ed.), *Theories of Ethics*, p. 75]. But this simply represents an explicit assimilation of commending, which is expressive, to recommending, which is directive, at the level of answer to a question of what to choose or to do in a particular circumstance.

23. Evaluations can be illocutions or psychological attitudes. In Vendler's jargon, there is, in the case of the verb *evaluate*, "leakage" from the mental domain to the domain of speech. See Vendler, *RC*, ch. 3, pp. 28, 34.

24. See Vendler, *RC*, ch. 2, pp. 19, 24; ch. 3, p. 34; Searle, CIA, pp. 18–19.

25. See Vendler, *RC*, ch. 2, pp. 16–19, 24; ch. 3, pp. 32–33.

26. See Vendler, *A & N*, ch. 3, pp. 35–36; *RC*, ch. 2, pp. 16–19, 24; Searle, CIA, pp. 16–17.

27. *How to Do Things with Words*, lecture 12, pp. 152, 161–62.

28. Searle goes wrong when he says "not just what do we state, claim, characterize, or assert, but how do we describe, call. . .", for *characterize* belongs in the second illocutionary list. He himself puts it there a few lines later on: "are all characteristically *statements*, in the making of

which we call, diagnose and describe, as well as accuse, identify and characterize'' (p. 20).

29. Contrast Searle, *Speech Acts (SA)*, 8.2, pp. 182 ff.

30. Compare Hare, *LM* 7.5, pp. 124–25; 11.1, pp. 164 ff; *FR* 10.1–2, pp. 186–91.

31. Compare Hare, *FR* 4.2, p. 53; 5.6, pp. 75 ff.

32. Construed subjunctively as ''It ought to be that I (should) leave at once''. See fn. 36 and the related discussion.

33. Compare Wittgenstein, in *Zettel*, at 51:

> Application of the imperative. Compare these orders:
>> Raise your arm
>> Imagine . . .
>> Work . . . out in your head
>> Consider . . .
>> Concentrate your attention on . . .
>> See this figure as a cube
>
> with these:
>
>> Intend. . .
>> Mean . . . by those words
>> Suspect that this is the case
>> Believe that it is so
>> Be of the firm conviction . . .
>> Remember that this happened
>> Hope for his return

Is *this* the difference, that the first are voluntary, the second involuntary mental movements? I may rather say that the verbs of the second group do not stand for actions. (Compare with this the order: ''Laugh heartily at this joke''). See too *Zettel*, 52.

34. Hare, *LM* 7.1, p. 111 (strawberry); *LM* 7.1, p. 112 (motor car); and *MSA*, p. 75 (movie).

35. See A. R. White, *Modal Thinking*, ch. 10, p. 140; and Roger Wertheimer, *The Significance of Sense*, ch. 1, pp. 19 ff.

36. White, *Modal Thinking*, ch. 10, pp. 139 ff. White writes: ''As with 'must', there are, however, two importantly different ways in which

'ought' modifies its main verb. 'Ought to V' may indicate either subjunctively 'ought to be that it (should) V' or indicatively 'ought to be that it does V'. Hence, the syntactical ambiguity of the sentence 'There ought to be a law against it' as said, on the one hand, by the recent victim of a confidence trick and, on the other, by a student looking through the Statute Book, or of 'The teachers ought to get a rise in salary', as, on the one hand, a prescription and, on the other, a prediction. Because almost any example of 'ought to V' could, with sufficient ingenuity, be taken either way, only the context will show which is meant. Normally, 'If one is tired, one ought to take a rest' would be an example of the subjunctive-governing use and 'If one takes a rest, one ought to wake refreshed' of the indicative-governing use'' (p. 139).

37. Compare Warnock, *Contemporary Moral Philosophy*, ch. 4, pp. 34–36, and *The Object of Morality*, ch. 8, pp. 125 ff. Wittgenstein's remark in *Philosophical Investigations*, at 593, is pertinent: "A main cause of philosophical disease—a one-sided diet: one nourishes one's thinking with only one kind of example".

CHAPTER THREE: Evaluatives, Volitives, Indicatives, and Evaluative Thinking

1. Compare D. R. Bell, "Imperatives and the Will'', *Proceedings of the Aristotelian Society* 66 (1965–66): 130; and Anthony Kenny, *Will, Freedom and Power*, ch. 3, pp. 29 ff.

2. See *LM* 2.5, p. 29; 3.4, p. 46; 11.1–5, passim; *FR* 4.3, pp. 54–55.

3. In Robert Binkley, Richard Bronaugh, and Ausonio Marras (eds.), *Agent, Action and Reason*, pp. 81–97.

4. The example is curious in the following way. The desire in question is meant to contrast with a mere "idle wish", that is, a wish expressible as an optative. Hare writes, "We might say that the latter is idle, unlike the former, because its expression, unlike an imperative, does not command any action" (pp. 89–90). But to have sugar in one's soup is not to perform an action, and so "Let me have sugar in my soup" is a curious imperative. It would seem better to characterize the relevant desire more fully as a desire to bring something about, or some such. Compare Kenny, *Action, Emotion and Will*, ch. 10, pp. 207–8, 210–11.

5. See John Searle, *Speech Acts (SA)* 3.4, p. 65; and "A Classification of Illocutionary Acts" (CIA), *Language in Society* 5 (1976): 4.

6. The self/other distinction is a generic *metaphysical* one; so, for example, my issuing a directive to *us*, and correspondingly, my intending or

wanting *us* to do something, represents a case of an *other*-person directive and volition.

7.   Compare H.-N. Castañeda, *Thinking and Doing*, ch. 6, pp. 154–55: "(A) The fundamental practical questions *Shall I do *A*?* and *What shall I do?*, without loss of self-identity, allow of two types of answer complementary to each other. The first type is the *prescriptive* answer that another may give: *Do *A* or *Don't do *A*. The second answer is the *intentional* one, the one that the agent himself must give: *I shall do *A* or *I shan't do *A*."

8.   Compare Gilbert Harman's remarks on the child's development of a "superego", *The Nature of Morality*, ch. 5, p. 60.

9.   In Anton C. Pegis (ed.), *The Wisdom of Catholicism*, p. 72.

10.   In Lawrence, *Love among the Haystacks, and Other Stories*, pp. 57–58.

11.   Note the identity switch at the end; the old man now makes believe that someone *else* has been offering *him* counsel. For further examples, see pp. 45, 55–56, 80–81, 83, 85, 89, 97, 107.

12.   It is an issue whether so-called self-addressed directive illocutions *ever* are *bona fide* or serious illocutions. Wittgenstein apparently thinks so (*Philosophical Investigations*, at 630). For a critical discussion, see Bell, "Imperatives and the Will", pp. 129–48. Castañeda accepts the view that one can command oneself to do something (although in the second or third person) (*Thinking and Doing*, p. 155). I think that *typical* examples of so-called self-addressed directives are most plausibly interpreted as cases wherein a person dissociates from himself in his imagination and imagines that he (or some part of himself) is talking to someone *else* (or another part of himself) in order to get *himself* to act in a certain way. Kenny, however, presents the following interesting case in *Will, Freedom and Power*, ch. 3. "The difficulty is not that one cannot give oneself orders: one can. (For example, a commander may give orders by posting a duty rota, on which his own name appears as well as others')" (p. 33). This unusual case suggests the following kind of amendment to what I have been saying: directive illocutions are essentially illocutions in which one person says to another, *or himself under an other-person description,* that he should do something, and the intentions or desires they count as expressing, and hence the intentions or desires imperatives are suitable for putting into words, are intentions or desires that someone else, *or oneself conceived as someone else,* should do something.

13.   Compare R. B. Braithwaite, A Review of Hare's *The Language of*

Morals, Mind 63 (1954): 257; and D. F. Pears, "Comments" in Binkley et al. (eds.), pp. 117–18.

14. In book 8, ch. 9, of *The Confessions* Augustine writes: "The mind commands the hand to be moved; and such readiness is there, that command is scarce distinct from obedience"—Pegis (ed.), p. 69. Compare Goethe in *Willkommen und Abschied:* "Es schlug mein Herz, geschwind zu Pferde! Es war getan fast eh gedacht" ("My heart beat: go quickly on horseback! It was done almost before the thought was over") Leonard Forster (ed.), *The Penguin Book of German Verse*, p. 196.

15. For the term *imperation* see "Wanting", pp. 95–96.

16. "Wanting" pp. 91–94, 96. Compare "The Freedom of the Will", *Proceedings of the Aristotelian Society* Supp. Vol. 25 (1951): 206 ff; *LM* 1.7, pp. 12 ff; Hare's review of Warnock's *Contemporary Moral Philosophy, Mind* 77 (1968): 437; and his review of Castañeda's *The Structure of Morality* in the *Journal of Philosophy* 73 (1976): 484–85.

17. See "The Freedom of the Will", pp. 210 ff; *LM* 2.5, p. 29; 3.4, p. 46; chs. 10–11, passim; "Wanting", pp. 92, 95–96; review of Castañeda's *The Structure of Morality*, pp. 484–85. Compare Warnock, *Contemporary Moral Philosophy*, ch. 4, pp. 30–32.

18. See Kenny, *Action, Emotion and Will*, chs. 10–11, pp. 203–39; and *Will, Freedom and Power*, ch. 3, pp. 29–45. Compare Geach's analysis of "*N* judges that such and such is the case "as" *N* says in-his-heart something to the same effect as (mentally utters): 'such and such is the case' " (*Mental Acts*, chs. 17–19, pp. 75–92; chs. 22–23, pp. 98–106). The "saying-in-the-heart" metaphor has, so to speak, a venerable tradition. Geach (*Mental Acts*, ch. 18, p. 80) and Kenny (*Action, Emotion and Will*, ch. 10, p. 207) quote examples from the Bible, and Anselm, in ch. 18 of *The Proslogion*, asks: "But how was it that the fool said in his heart something which could not be thought? And how was it that he was unable to think what he said in his heart? For, to say something in one's heart and to think are one and the same thing" [Pegis (ed.), p. 216]. The metaphor, however, generates a puzzle. Compare Wittgenstein, in *Philosophical Investigations*, at 658: "Suppose we expressed the fact that a man had an intention by saying "He as it were said to himself 'I will . . .' " That is the picture. And now I want to know: how does one employ the expression "as it were to say something to oneself"? For it does not mean: to say something to oneself."

19. This is the line Searle takes (see CIA, p. 11). Compare Castañeda: "The use of an imperative carries with it the idea or intention that the im-

perative is to participate, however small this participation may be, in a causal chain of events which will terminate with the agent's doing the action in question. We shall refer to this typical feature of imperatives as the *causal intention* or the *pushing aspect* of issued imperatives'' (*Thinking and Doing*, pp. 291–92).

20.   Compare ''Wanting'', pp. 92–93: ''However, it ought to be clear at least that it is not true of commands in general that the person who issues them is, ex vi termini, trying to get people to do the things specified. The sadistic schoolmaster, who commands his boys to keep silent in the hope that this will cause them to talk so that he can beat them, is still commanding or telling them to keep quiet.'' See also Les Holborow, ''The Commitment Fallacy'', *Noûs* 5 (1971): 392.

21.   Pears' phrase. See his ''Comments'' in Binkley et al. (eds.), p. 118.

22.   For examples of commissives see Austin, *How to Do Things with Words*, lecture 12, pp. 156–57; Vendler, *RC*, ch. 2, pp. 19–20; ch. 3, pp. 34–35; Searle, *CIA*, pp. 7, 11.

23.   H. W. Fowler, *A Dictionary of Modern English Usage*, 2d ed., p. 549. Contrast Castañeda's use of ''I shall'' for expressions of intention and ''I will'' for predictions (*Thinking and Doing*, ch. 2, pp. 41–42).

24.   See Pears, ''Comments'', in Binkley et al. (eds.), pp. 113–14, 122, 123–24. For Pears, ''I will do *A*'' ''expresses a greater degree of determination'' than ''I shall do *A*'' (p. 123).

25.   Kenny fails to appreciate this in his reply to Pears in *Will, Freedom and Power*, ch. 3. Kenny says: ''I agree that 'I will do *A*' and 'I intend to do *A*' may be used to give information as well as to express an intention and that it may sometimes be difficult to tell which of the two a speaker is doing and that sometimes he may be doing both at once. My claim is only that insofar as 'I will do *A*' is an expression of intention it can be expressed in a philosophically less misleading way as 'Let me do *A*'; and insofar as it is a genuine report, it is tantamount, on the imperative theory, to 'I have said in my heart, 'Let me do *A*' '' (p. 34).

26.   See Searle, ''Indirect Speech Acts'' (hereafter ISA) in Peter Cole and Jerry L. Morgan (eds.), *Syntax and Semantics: Speech Acts* 3, pp. 79 ff.

27.   For Searle on propositional content, see *SA* 2.4, pp. 29 ff; also ISA, p. 71.

28.   For the primary performative/explicit performative contrast, see Austin, *How to Do Things with Words*, lecture 6, pp. 69 ff, passim. Compare Hare, ''Austin's Distinction between Locutionary and Illocutionary Acts'' in *Practical Inferences*, pp. 102–3.

29. See Vendler, *A & N*, ch. 4, pp. 56, 59–61; *RC*, ch. 2, pp. 19–20, 24, 34–35; Searle, CIA, pp. 17–18.

30. Compare Castañeda, *Thinking and Doing*, ch. 6, pp. 154–55.

31. See *LM* 2.2, pp. 19–20; 11.2–3, pp. 168–72; *FR* 4.3, pp. 54–55; "Wanting", p. 85 et passim (but note p. 94).

32. In Boris Ford (ed.), *From Donne to Marvell: The Pelican Guide to English Literature* 3, p. 104.

33. Compare S. Hampshire, *Thought and Action*, ch. 2, p. 134; ch. 3, pp. 182–83; and Pears, "Comments", p. 124.

34. See Vendler, *A & N*, ch. 4, pp. 56, 59; *RC*, ch. 2, pp. 19–20; Searle, CIA, p. 17. Sometimes commissive verbs are followed by an accusative and infinitive construction. But the difference between "*N* promises *(M)* to do *x*" and "*N* orders *M* to do *x*" is that the accusative is deleteable in the former.

35. It is sometimes challenged that we make statements about ourselves when we say things like "I want (desire) to do *x*", "I intend to do *x*", and so on. Austin, for example, lists *intend* and *wish* ["(in its strict performative use)", he says] as commissive and behabitive illocutionary verbs, respectively (*How to Do Things with Words*, lecture 12, pp. 156, 159); and he hesitantly adds *doubt, know,* and *believe* to his list of expositives (lecture 12, p. 161). This gives the unfortunate impression that he thinks sentences like "I intend to do *x*" are explicit performatives like "I promise to do *x*". But they clearly are not. I note Searle's observations: "Take 'intend': it is clearly not performative. Saying 'I intend' is not intending; nor in the third person does it name an illocutionary act: 'He intended . . .' does not report a speech act. Of course there is an illocutionary act of *expressing an intention*, but the illocutionary verb phrase is: 'express an intention', not 'intend'. Intending is never a speech act; expressing an intention usually, but not always, is" (CIA, p. 8). Sometimes what is claimed is that "I want to do *x*", "I intend to do *x*", and so on, are (at least sometimes) not *statements* but rather *expressions of* desires, intentions, etc. (Compare Kenny, *Action, Emotion and Will*, ch. 11, pp. 213–41, esp. 218). Sometimes it is this kind of thing which is stressed: "I believe that such and such is the case" is not a statement about my mind but a tentative assertion of "Such and such is the case", just as "I want you to do *x*" is not a statement about my mind but a polite way of saying to you "Do *x*", and so on. (Compare Hare *LM* 1.3, p. 6; Austin, "Other Minds", in J. O. Urmson and G. J. Warnock (eds.), *Philosophical Papers*, pp. 98 ff). But I think that good reason for holding that one of the things someone does when he says something like "I want (desire) to do *x*", "I intend to do *x*",

etc., is make a statement about himself, is that the speaker, in such cases, can be reported as saying that he wants (desires) to do x, intends to do x, and so forth. This contrasts with cases where someone says something like "I will (shall) do x" (intentive expression of intention). It also contrasts with genuine explicit performative cases; for, whereas someone who says "I want to do x" can be reported as saying he wants to, someone who says "I promise to do x" is correctly reported as promising to do x, not as saying he promises to do x.

36. David Gauthier, "Comments", in *Agent, Action and Reason*, ed. Binkley, pp. 102–103.

37. See Chapter 2, beginning of Sec. A.

38. Compare Chapter 2, sec. 5, above.

39. See: A. J. Ayer, *Language, Truth and Logic*, ch. 6, pp. 107 ff; C. L. Stevenson, "The Emotive Meaning of Ethical Terms", in *Contemporary Ethical Theory*, ed. Joseph Margolis, pp. 81 ff; G. Harman, *The Nature of Morality*, chs. 3–4, pp. 27 ff.

40. See Hare, *LM* 1.5, pp. 9–10; 9.2, pp. 140–44. Compare Warnock, *Contemporary Moral Philosophy*, ch. 3, pp. 26–29.

41. Compare A. R. White on "intellectual feelings" in *The Philosophy of Mind*, ch. 5, pp. 105–107.

CHAPTER FOUR: Value and Reason

1. See Chapter 1, end of sec. 1 and opening of sec. 5.

2. See Chapter 1, first pages of sec. 6.

3. See Chapter 1, first two pages of sec. 5, esp. fn. 44.

4. Compare Grice, *The Gounds of Moral Judgement*, ch. 5, pp. 188–89; Searle, *Speech Acts* 6.5, p. 152; White, *Modal Thinking*, ch. 11, p. 178; J. L. Mackie, *Ethics*, ch. 2, pp. 55 ff; Harman, *The Nature of Morality*, ch. 2, pp. 14 ff; J. O. Urmson, "On Grading" in Antony Flew (ed.), *Logic and Language* (2d series), ch. 9, pp. 159–86.

5. Compare von Wright, *The Varieties of Goodness* (hereafter *VG*), ch. 1, p. 12 ff; for hedonic examples, see ch. 4, pp. 63 ff.

6. On the contrast between the meaning (or force) and criteria of terms, see Stephen Toulmin, *The Uses of Argument*, ch. 1, pp. 30 ff; White, *Modal Thinking*, ch. 11, pp. 178–79. Compare Hare, *LM* 6, pp. 94 ff; 7.3, pp. 117–18.

7. Compare von Wright, *VG*, ch. 2, pp. 20 ff; and Hare, *LM* 6.4, pp. 99 ff.

8. Von Wright's term. See *VG*, ch. 2, pp. 25–26.

9. See Vendler, *Adjectives and Nominalizations*, ch. 4, pp. 63–65; ch. 6, pp. 103–4; and "The Grammar of Goodness" in his *Linguistics in Philosophy*, pp. 186 ff.

10. Perhaps more strictly: *valuable enough*. For to say that something is good enough would seem, more accurately, to come to saying that it possesses in sufficient degree that characteristic (or set of characteristics) the having of which in great or high degree would make it good.

11. Note that prudential and altruistic rightness are subvarieties of utilitarian rightness, just as prudential and altruistic goodness are subvarieties of utilitarian goodness. Thus the right thing for one to do for oneself—the action on one's part which is sufficiently beneficial to oneself—is the thing for one to do which is sufficiently useful for promoting one's well-being.

12. Compare Alan Montefiore, " 'Ought' and 'Can' ", *Philosophical Quarterly* 8 (1958): 39; Kurt Baier, *The Moral Point of View*, ch. 3, pp. 85 ff; B. J. Diggs, "A Technical Ought", *Mind* 69 (1960): 302; David Gauthier, *Practical Reasoning*, ch. 2, pp. 10 ff; Aaron Sloman, " 'Ought' and 'Better' ", *Mind* 79 (1970): 385–94; Joseph Margolis, *Values and Conduct*, chs. 3–5, pp. 57–111.

13. Prudential oughtness, like altruistic oughtness, is, in fact, a species of utilitarian oughtness (see fn. 11 above): what I ought to do so far as I go (that is, what is in my greatest interest to do) is what I ought to do in order to promote my own interest (what is most useful for me to do in order to promote my own interest).

14. Compare White, *Modal Thinking (MT)*, ch. 10, pp. 140–41. See too ch. 7, pp. 100–1.

15. *Ethics*, ch. 1, p. 9; *The Definition of Good*; ch. 4, pp. 123–4. Compare W. D. Ross, *The Right and the Good*, ch. 1, pp. 1–15; and Hare, *LM*, 10.1, pp. 151–153; 12.2, pp. 181 ff.

16. Compare D. G. Brown, *Action*, ch. 3, pp. 101–2.

17. For the construal of *ought* in terms of the concept of reason, compare Kurt Baier, ch. 3, pp. 85 ff; ch. 9, pp. 222 ff; Grice, ch. 1, pp. 24 ff; ch. 2, pp. 42 ff; ch. 3, pp. 93 ff, 131 ff; ch. 4, pp. 172 ff; Roy Edgley, *Reason in Theory and Practice*, 4.10, pp. 132 ff, and "Hume's Law", *Proceedings of the Aristotelian Society* Supp. Vol. 44 (1970): 112 ff; Grice, "Hume's Law", ibid., pp. 92–93; D. A. J. Richards, *A Theory of Reasons for Action*, ch. 4,

pp. 52 ff; ch. 12, pp. 212 ff, esp. 219 ff; Harman, ch. 10, pp. 115 ff; Mackie, ch. 3, pp. 73 ff. Contrast White, ch. 10, pp. 141–42; see too ch. 7, p. 101.

CHAPTER FIVE: Present Reason for Acting and Prior Volition

1. I am appealing here to an intuition that, I trust, is shared. Just *why* judgements about reasons for acting of one kind rather than another (e.g., perhaps, about moral and prudential reasons rather than legal reasons or reasons of etiquette) can serve as ultimate justifying grounds for all-out summary judgements about reasons for acting is notoriously obscure. For my part, I offer no theory of practical rationality in this essay.

2. See "Reasons for Action and Desires" in *Virtues and Vices* (hereafter *VV*), pp. 148 ff.

3. Ibid., pp. 151 ff. See too Foot's articles, "Morality as a System of Hypothetical Imperatives" in *VV*, pp. 157–73; "A Reply to Professor Frankena," in ibid., pp. 174–80; " 'Is Morality a System of Hypothetical Imperatives?' A Reply to Mr. Holmes", *Analysis* 35 (1974–75): 53–56. For discussion of Foot, see Robert L. Holmes, "Is Morality a System of Hypothetical Imperatives?" *Analysis* 34 (1973–74): 96–100, and "Philippa Foot on Hypothetical Imperatives", *Analysis* 36 (1975–76): 199–200; Winston Nesbitt, "Categorical Imperatives: A Defense", *Philosophical Review* 86 (1977): 217–25; D. Z. Phillips, "In Search of the Moral 'Must': Mrs. Foot's Fugitive Thought", *Philosophical Quarterly* 27 (1977): 140–57; John McDowell and I. C. McFetridge, "Are Moral Requirements Hypothetical Imperatives?" *Proceedings of the Aristotelian Society* Supp. Vol. 52 (1978): 13–42.

4. Ch. 13, p. 152. Compare ch. 11, pp. 132–33; ch. 13, p. 162.

5. See Chapter 4 above, beginning of sec. 3.

6. See "Reasons for Action and Desires" in *VV*, pp. 150 ff; "Morality as a System of Hypothetical Imperatives," ibid., pp. 159 ff, esp. 161; and " 'Is Morality a System of Hypothetical Imperatives?' A Reply to Mr. Holmes", *Analysis* 35 (1974–75): 53 ff.

7. Compare Winston Nesbitt, "Categorical Imperatives: A Defense", *Philosophical Review* 86 (1971): 217–18; Robert L. Holmes, "Is Morality a System of Hypothetical Imperatives?", *Analysis* 34 (1973–74): 98–99; Robert L. Holmes, "Philippa Foot on Hypothetical Imperatives", *Analysis* 36 (1975–76): 199–200.

8. Philosophers sometimes talk of "justifying" and "motivating" reasons as though there were two senses of *reason*, one evaluative and the

other motivational. [See William Frankena, "Obligation and Motivation in Recent Moral Philosophy" in A. I. Melden (ed.), *Essays in Moral Philosophy*, pp. 44 ff; and Holmes, two articles, one in *Analysis* 34 (1973–74): 98, and the other in *Analysis* 36 (1975–76): 199–200.] But Thomas Nagel is right that we are *not* "faced with two disparate concepts finding refuge in a single word". (See Nagel, *The Possibility of Altruism*, ch. 3, p. 15. Compare Grice, *The Grounds of Moral Judgement*, ch. 1, pp. 8 ff.) For *N's* reason for acting is something *N takes* to be *a* reason for him to act. [Compare A. Phillips Griffiths and Donald McQueen, "Beliefs and Reasons for Belief", *Proceedings of the Aristotelian Society* Supp. Vol. 47 (1973): 53–86; Don Locke, "Reasons, Wants and Causes", *American Philosophical Quarterly* 11 (1974): 170 ff.]

9.   See Chapter 1 above, sec. 6, opening pages. Compare Grice, ch. 1, p. 12: "The formula *no reason without a desire* is false. But the formula *no motive without a desire* is true". See Grice's discussion, pp. 10 ff.

10.   Warnock rejects this theory. See ibid., ch. 3, pp. 29 ff. See too Mackie, ch. 6, pp. 125 ff.

11.   See Grice, ch. 3, pp. 93 ff. Grice distinguishes two segments of morality: basic and ultra. See ch. 2, pp. 36–37; ch. 4, pp. 155 ff. On the relation between rule utilitarianism and his contract theory, see Grice, ch. 5, pp. 197–98.

12.   In addition to selecting prima facie principles, says Hare, critical thinking has the role of resolving conflicts between them (see *MrT* 3.3, pp. 49 ff). With respect to the latter, Hare writes:

> What critical thinking has to do is to find a moral judgement which the thinker is prepared to make about this conflict-situation and is also prepared to make about all the other similar situations. Since these will include situations in which he occupies, respectively, the positions of all the other parties in the actual situation, no judgement will be acceptable to him which does not do the best, all in all, for all the parties. Thus the logical apparatus of universal prescriptivism, if we understand what we are saying when we make moral judgements, will lead us in critical thinking (without relying on any substantial moral intuitions) to make judgements which are the same as a careful act-utilitarian would make (*MrT* 2.6, pp. 42–43).

13.   Compare Warnock, *The Object of Morality*, ch. 9, pp. 150 ff; Hare, *MrT* 5.2, pp. 90–91.

14.   See my discussion, in sec. 2, below.

15.   See Warnock, ch. 5, pp. 53 ff. For the distinction between principles and rules, see Marcus G. Singer, "Moral Rules and Principles", in Melden (ed.), *Essays in Moral Philosophy*, pp. 160–97; and David A. J. Richards, *A Theory of Reasons for Action*, ch. 2, pp. 11 ff.

16.   See Richards on *N's* and *the* principles, ibid., ch. 2, pp. 11 ff. Such *meta-principle* judgements which relativise value or reason to (meeting the requirements of) certain principles should alert us to the difference between principles—or better, the attitudes they are apt for expressing—and evaluations. Volitionist internalists like Hare assimilate moral principles, or the corresponding attitudes, to moral evaluations. Principles are imperatives and correspond to appropriate volitions. The language of assent or subscription to principles is, of course, intentive. Evaluations are cognitions, as the exclusive indicativity of corresponding evaluatives reveals. (Compare Richards, ibid., ch. 2, pp. 17 ff; ch. 4, pp. 49 ff; ch. 12, pp. 212 ff.)

17.   Compare his discussion "The Natural Attitude of Rationality", ibid., ch. 5., pp. 63 ff.

18.   Sometimes Kant characterizes a hypothetical imperative as saying that an action is *good* for a purpose; other times he characterizes it as saying that an action is *necessary* for a purpose.

19.   Kant, like many others, does not distinguish between one's good or interest or well-being, on the one hand, and one's happiness, on the other (see *FP*, pp. 33 ff). But the two are clearly different. Happiness *supervenes* upon the possession of one's good as *its enjoyment*. This is like the relation between being healthy and feeling well: feeling well is the *enjoyment of* health. (Compare von Wright, *VG*, ch. 5, pp. 86 ff, esp. 92 ff.)

20.   *Journal of Philosophy* 76 (1979): 738–53.

21.   Stocker says, it will be noted, that helping and harming others can be the *direct and proper* objects of desires and appetites. The intention is clear: the desire to help or to harm another need not be construed as intermediate with respect to some further desire, in particular some further selfish desire. In the next paragraph, Stocker comments, "Given such moods and circumstances, harming another can be the proper and direct object of attraction. There is no need to posit another object, especially not an egoistic object like pleasure, power over others, showing oneself powerful, getting things to go one's own way, getting revenge" (p. 748).

22.   Page numbers hereafter cited in the text refer to the 1971 Fontana edition of *The Woman Destroyed*.

23.   That is to say: examples that *make sense* and ring true to how it *actually or really could be* for us.

24. For example, in Jean Genet's *Funeral Rites* (pp. 152–53), there is the following portrayal of the self-indifference of someone benumbed by immense grief:

> He put his grimy, though broad and shapely, hand on the maid's knees, which were covered by the black dress. She was paralyzed with such indifference that she would have let her throat be slit without thinking of any reproach but the following: "Well, well, so my time has come".
> The man grew bolder. He put his arm around her waist. She made no movement to shake him off. In view of what seemed to be willingness on her part, the second gravedigger regretted not being in on the fun, and he sat down on the stone on the other side of the maid.
> "Ah, she's a very nice little girl", he said laughingly. And he put his arm around the maid's neck and pulled her to him, against his chest. No doubt an entreaty arose within her, but she found no word to formulate it. The sudden boldness of his mate excited the first fellow, who leaned over and kissed her on the cheek. Both men laughed, grew still bolder, and kept pawing her. Beside her little daughter's fresh grave, she allowed them to mistreat her, to open her dress, to stroke and fondle her poor, indifferent pussy. Grief made her insensitive to everything, to her grief itself. She saw herself at the end of her rope, that is, on the point of flying away from the earth once and for all. And that grief which transcended itself was due not only to her daughter's death, it was the sum of all her miseries as a woman and her miseries as a housemaid, of all the human miseries that overwhelmed her that day because a ceremony, which, moreover, was meant to do so, had extracted all those miseries from her person in which they were scattered.

Thus far I have concentrated on "dark" examples, that is, examples in which, to adapt André Gide's words, various depressions "interpose themselves between desire and life" so that "we are aware of things, but they fail to move us" (*Isabelle*, pp. 124–25). But we can, of course, become indifferent to ourselves, as we can become indifferent to others, in other ways. Curiosity, for example, can make us indifferent to our own welfare. In *So Be It, or The Chips Are Down* (pp. 81 ff), Gide writes:

> In so-called real life I am most often prudent and cautious; but at times the demon of curiosity carries the day (I should say "carries

me away'') and makes me careless of danger. Like that night when, very late, I had ventured onto the stairs of the Algiers harbour in pursuit of two young Arabs who seemed to me very strange. A very well-dressed gentleman—and certainly with a charitable intention—whispered in quite distinct and quite distinguished voice (we were still on the upper quay, but it was obvious that I was on the point of going down toward the ill-lighted docks) as I passed near him (but what was he himself doing on that deserted quay?): "Watch out, Sir; what you are doing is extremely dangerous". I think I said "Thank you" to him as I raised my hat and lowered my embarrassed face. But when I raised my face the two boys had disappeared. And perhaps, after all, that stranger saved my life.

Another night, instead of two kids, it was two strapping fellows. . . .

Then there is self-indifference born of that kind of mood of defiant or rebellious perversity celebrated by Dostoyevsky in *Notes from Underground* (pp. 29 ff):

But all these are golden daydreams. Tell me, who was it who first declared, proclaiming it to the whole world, that a man does evil only because he does not know his real interests, and if he is enlightened and has his eyes opened to his own best and normal interests, man will cease to do evil and at once become virtuous and noble, because when he is enlightened and understands what will really benefit him he will see his own best interest in virtue, and since it is well known that no man can knowingly act against his best interests, consequently he will inevitably, so to speak, begin to do good. Oh, what a baby! Oh, what a pure innocent child! To begin with, when in all those thousands of years have men acted solely in their own interests? What about all those millions of incidents testifying to the fact that men have *knowingly*, that is in full understanding of their own best interests, put them in the background and taken a perilous and uncertain course not because anybody or anything drove them to it, but simply and solely because they did not choose to follow the appointed road, as it were, but wilfully and obstinately preferred to pursue a perverse and difficult path almost lost in the darkness?

Gide points to yet another possibility in *If It Die* (pp. 301–2). He records that, on the death of his mother, he experienced "a kind of moral intoxication which led me to commit the most ill-considered acts . . . a sort of heady abnegation''. In this mood he disposed of his mother's effects without thought for himself and, despite his homosexuality, became engaged to Emmanuèle—''I should have thought all prudence cowardly'', Gide writes, ''cowardly all idea of danger . . . I was dazzled as by a blaze of azure''.

Bibliography

Alston, William. "Wants, Actions and Causal Explanation" (with comments by Keith Lehrer and Rejoinder) in Hector-Neri Castañeda (ed.), *Intentionality, Minds and Perception*. Detroit: Wayne State University Press, 1967, pp. 301-56.

Anscombe, G. E. M. *Intention*. 2d Ed. Oxford: Basil Blackwell, 1963.

———. "Thought and Action in Aristotle" in Renford Bambrough(ed.), *New Essays on Plato and Aristotle*. London: Routledge and Kegan Paul, 1965, pp. 143-58.

———. "Modern Moral Philosophy", in W. D. Hudson (ed.), *The Is-Ought Question*. London: Macmillan, 1969, pp. 175-95.

Anselm, *The Proslogion*, in Anton C. Pegis (ed.), *The Wisdom of Catholicism*. London: Michael Joseph, 1950, pp. 211-32.

Aquinas, Thomas. *Summa Theologiae* 44 (*Well-Tempered Passion*, 2a 2ae, 155-70). Cambridge: Blackfriars, 1972.

Aristotle. *Aristotle's Ethics*. Edited and translated by John Warrington. London: J.M. Dent, Everyman's Library, 1970.

Armstrong, D. M. *Belief, Truth and Knowledge*. London: Cambridge University Press, 1973.

Audi, Robert. "The Concept of Wanting", *Philosophical Studies* 24 (1973): 1-21.

———. "Weakness of Will and Practical Judgment". *Noûs* 13 (1979): 173-76.

———. "A Theory of Practical Reasoning", *American Philosophical Quarterly* 19 (1982): 25-39.

Augustine. *The Confessions*, in Anton C. Pegis (ed.), *The Wisdon of Catholicism*. London: Michael Joseph, 1950, pp. 64-123.

Austin, J. L. *How to Do Things with Words*. Oxford: Oxford University Press, 1962.

——. "Other Minds", pp. 76–116, and "A Plea for Excuses", pp. 175–204, in J.O. Urmson and G.J. Warnock (eds.), *Philosophical Papers*. 2d Ed. Oxford: Oxford University Press, 1970.

Ayer, A. J. *Language, Truth and Logic*. London: Victor Gollancz, 1967.

Baier, Kurt. *The Moral Point of View: A Rational Basis of Ethics*. Ithaca, N.Y.: Cornell University Press, 1958.

Bambrough, J. Renford. "Socratic Paradox", *Philosophical Quarterly* 10 (1960): 289–300.

Bell, D. R. "Imperatives and the Will", *Proceedings of the Aristotelian Society* 66 (1965–66): 129–48.

Bellow, Saul. *Seize the Day*. Harmondsworth, Middlesex: Penguin Books, 1977.

Benacerraf, Paul. "Comments", in C. D. Rollins (ed.), *Knowledge and Experience*. Pittsburgh: University of Pittsburgh Press, 1966, pp. 43–49.

Benson, John. "Wants, Desires and Deliberation", pp. 200–15, and "Further Thoughts on Oughts and Wants", pp. 226–32, in Geoffrey Mortimore (ed.), *Weakness of Will*. London: Macmillan, 1971.

Bond, E. J. "Reasons, Wants and Values", *Canadian Journal of Philosophy* 3 (1974): 333–47).

Braithwaite, R. B. Review of R. M. Hare's *The Language of Morals*, *Mind* 63 (1954): pp. 249–62.

Brandom, Robert. "Points of View and Practical Reasoning", *Canadian Journal of Philosophy* 12 (1982): 321–33.

Brandt, Richard, and Jaegwon Kim. "Wants as Explanations of Action", *Journal of Philosophy* 60 (1963): 425–35.

Brandt, Richard. A Review of R. M. Hare's *Freedom and Reason*, *Journal of Philosophy* 61 (1964): 139–50.

Bratman, Michael. "Practical Reasoning and Weakness of the Will", *Noûs* 13 (1979): 153–71.

Brown, D. G. *Action*. London: George Allen and Unwin, 1968.

Campbell, C. A. "The Psychology of Effort of Will", *Proceedings of the Aristotelian Society* 40 (1939–40): 49–74.

Castañeda, Hector-Neri. "Imperatives, Decisions, and 'Oughts': A Logico-Metaphysical Investigation" in Castañeda and George Nakhnikian (eds.), *Morality and the Language of Conduct*. Detroit: Wayne State University Press, 1963, pp. 219–29.

——. *Thinking and Doing*. Dordrecht: D. Reidel, 1975.

Chisholm, Roderick M. "Supererogation and Offence: A Conceptual Scheme for Ethics", *Ratio* 5 (1963): 1–14.

——. "The Structure of Intention", *Journal of Philosophy* 67 (1970): 633–47.

Churchland, Paul M. "The Logical Character of Action-Explanations", *Philosophical Review* 79 (1970): 214–36.

Cohen, L. Jonathan. "Do Illocutionary Forces Exist?" *Philosophical Quarterly* 14 (1964): 118–37.

Cooper, Neil. "Oughts and Wants" pp. 190–99, and "Further Thoughts on Oughts and Wants", pp. 216–25, in Geoffrey Mortimore (ed.), *Weakness of Will*. London: Macmillan, 1971.

Crombie, I. M. *An Examination of Plato's Doctrines*. Vol. 1, *Plato on Man and Society*. London: Routledge and Kegan Paul, 1962.

Darwall, Stephen L. "Nagel's Argument for Altruism", *Philosophical Studies* 25 (1974): 125–30.

Daveney, T. F. "Wanting", *Philosophical Quarterly* 11 (1961): 135–44.

——. "Choosing", *Mind* 73 (1964): 515–26.

Davidson, Donald. "Actions, Reasons, and Causes", pp. 2–19. "Freedom to Act", pp. 63–81. "How Is Weakness of Will Possible?" pp. 21–42. "Intending", pp. 83–102. In Davidson (ed.), *Essays on Actions and Events*. Oxford: Oxford University Press, 1980.

——. "Paradoxes of Irrationality", in Richard Wollheim and James Hopkins (eds.), *Philosophical Essays on Freud*. Cambridge: Cambridge University Press, 1982, pp. 289–305.

De Beauvoir, Simone. *The Woman Destroyed*. Translated by Patrick O'Brien. London: William Collins Sons, Fontana Books, 1971.

Diggs, B. J. "A Technical Ought", *Mind* 69 (1960): 301–17.

Donagan, Alan. "Alternative Historical Explanations and Their Verification", *Monist* 53 (1969): 58–89.

Donleavy, J. P. *The Saddest Summer of Samuel S*. Harmondsworth, Middlesex: Penguin Books, 1966.

Dostoyevsky, Fyodor. *Notes from Underground* and *The Double*. Translated by Jessie Coulson. Harmondsworth, Middlesex: Penguin Books, 1972.

Edgley, Roy. "Practical Reason", *Mind* 74 (1965): 174–91.

——. *Reason in Theory and Practice*. London: Hutchinson, 1969.

——. "Hume's Law", *Proceedings of the Aristotelian Society* Supp. Vol. 44 (1970): 105–19.

Edwards, Rem B. "Is Choice Determined by the 'Strongest Motive'?" *American Philosophical Quarterly* 4 (1967): 72–78.

Evans, Donald. "Moral Weakness", *Philosophy* 50 (1975): 295–310.

Evans, J. L. "Choice", *Philosophical Quarterly* 5 (1955): 303–315.

———. "Error and the Will", *Philosophy* 38 (1963): 136–48.

Ewing, A. C. *The Definition of Good*. New York: Macmillan, 1947.

———. *Ethics*. London: English Universities Press, 1953.

Falk, W. D. "Obligation and Rightness", *Philosophy* 20 (1945): 129–47.

———. " 'Ought' and Motivation", *Proceedings of the Aristotelian Society* 48 (1947–48): 111–38.

———. "Action-guiding Reasons", *Journal of Philosophy* 60 (1963): 702–18.

———. "Hume on Practical Reason", *Philosophical Studies* 27 (1975): 1–18.

Findlay, J. N. *Values and Intentions*. London: George Allen and Unwin, 1961.

Fingarette, Herbert. *Self-deception*. London: Routledge and Kegan Paul, 1969.

Fleming, Bruce Noel. "On Intention", *Philosophical Review* 73 (1964): 301–20.

Foley, Richard. "Prudence and the Desire Theory of Reasons", *Journal of Value Inquiry* 12 (1978): 68–73.

Foot, Philippa. "When Is a Principle a Moral Principle?" *Proceedings of the Aristotelian Society* Supp. Vol. 28 (1954): 95–110.

———. "Moral Arguments", *Mind* 67 (1958): 502–13.

———. "Moral Beliefs", in Foot (ed.), *Theories of Ethics*. Oxford: Oxford University Press, 1967, pp. 83–100.

———. "Goodness and Choice", in W. D. Hudson (ed.), *The Is-Ought Question*. London: Macmillan, 1969, pp. 214–27.

———. " 'Is Morality a System of Hypothetical Imperatives?' A Reply to Mr. Holmes", *Analysis* 35 (1974–75): 53–56.

———. "Reasons for Action and Desires", pp. 148–56. "Morality as a System of Hypothetical Imperatives", pp. 157–73. "A Reply to Professor Frankena", pp. 174–80. In Foot, *Virtues and Vices and Other Essays in Moral Philosophy*. Oxford, Basil Blackwell, 1978.

Ford, Boris (ed.). *From Donne to Marvell. The Pelican Guide to English Literature* 3. Harmondsworth, Middlesex: Penguin Books, 1963.

Forster, Leonard (ed.). *The Penguin Book of German Verse*. Harmondsworth, Middlesex: Penguin Books, 1966.

Fowler, H. W. *A Dictionary of Modern English Usage*. 2d Ed., revised by Sir Ernest Gowers. Oxford: Oxford University Press, 1965.

Frankena, William K. "Obligation and Motivation", in A. I. Melden (ed.), *Essays in Moral Philosophy*. Seattle: University of Washington Press, 1958, pp. 40–81.

Franks, D. S. "Choice", *Proceedings of the Aristotelian Society* 34 (1933–34): 269–94.

Fraser, Bruce. "Hedged Performatives", in P. Cole and Jerry L. Morgan (eds.), *Syntax and Semantics* 3. London: Academic Press, 1975, pp. 187–210.

Galligan, Edward M. "Irwin on Aristotle", *Journal of Philosophy* 72 (1975): 579–80.

Gardiner, Patrick. "Error, Faith and Self-deception", *Proceedings of the Aristotelian Society* 70 (1969–70): 221–43.

———. "On Assenting to a Moral Principle", in Geoffrey Mortimore (ed.), *Weakness of Will*. London: Macmillan, 1971, pp. 100–17.

Gauthier, David P. *Practical Reasoning*. Oxford: Oxford University Press, 1963.

———. "Comments", in Robert Binkley, Richard Bronaugh, Ausonio Marras (eds.), *Agent, Action, and Reason*. Toronto: University of Toronto Press, 1971, pp. 98–108.

Geach, Peter. *Mental Acts*. London: Routledge and Kegan Paul, 1971.

———. "Ascriptivism", *Philosophical Review* 69 (1960): 221–25.

———. "Assertion", *Philosophical Review* 74 (1965): 449–65.

———. "Good and Evil", in Philippa Foot (ed.), *Theories of Ethics*. Oxford: Oxford University Press, 1967, pp. 64–73.

Genet, Jean. *Funeral Rites*. St. Albans, Hertfordshire: Panther Books, 1973.

———. *The Thief's Journal*. Harmondsworth, Middlesex: Penguin Books, 1975.

Gewirth, Alan. "The Normative Structure of Action", *Review of Metaphysics* 25 (1971–72): 238–61.

Gibbs, Benjamin. "Virtue and Reason", *Proceedings of the Aristotelian Society* Supp. Vol. 48 (1974): 23–41.

Gide, André. *The Counterfeiters*. Translated by Dorothy Bussy. New York: Alfred A. Knopf, 1947.

———. *If It Die*. Translated by Dorothy Bussy. Harmondsworth, Middlesex: Penguin Books, 1957.

———. *So Be It, or The Chips Are Down.* Translated by Justin O'Brien. London: Chatto and Windus, 1960.

———. *La Symphonie pastorale* and *Isabelle.* Translated by Dorothy Bussy. Harmondsworth, Middlesex: Penguin Books, 1969.

———. *The Vatican Cellars.* Translated by Dorothy Bussy. Harmondsworth, Middlesex: Penguin Books, 1969.

Glasgow, W. D. "On Choosing", *Analysis* 17 (1956–57): 135–39.

———. "The Concept of Choosing", *Analysis* 20 (1959–60): 63–67.

Goldman, Alvin I. *A Theory of Human Action.* Englewood Cliffs, N.J.: Prentice-Hall, 1970.

Grice, G. R. *The Grounds of Moral Judgement.* Cambridge: Cambridge University Press, 1967.

———. "Hume's Law", *Proceedings of the Aristotelian Society* Supp. Vol. 44 (1970): 89–103.

Hampshire, Stuart. *Thought and Action.* London: Chatto and Windus, 1959.

———. "A Reply to Walsh on *Thought and Action*", *Journal of Philosophy* 60 (1963): 410–24.

———. *Freedom of the Individual.* Expanded Edition. Princeton, N.J.: Princeton University Press, 1975.

Hardie, W. F. R. "Aristotle on Moral Weakness", in Geoffrey Mortimore (ed.), *Weakness of Will.* London: Macmillan, 1971, pp. 69–94.

Hare, R. M. "The Freedom of the Will", *Proceedings of the Aristotelian Society* Supp. Vol. 25 (1951): 201–16.

———. *The Language of Morals.* Oxford: Oxford University Press, 1952.

———. Review of *Ethics* by P.H. Nowell-Smith, *Philosophy* 31 (1956): 89–92.

———. *Freedom and Reason.* Oxford: Oxford University Press, 1963.

———. "Geach: Good and Evil", in Philippa Foot (ed.), *Theories of Ethics.* Oxford: Oxford University Press, 1967, pp. 74–82.

———. Critical Review of *Contemporary Moral Philosophy* by G. J. Warnock, *Mind* 77 (1968): 436–40.

———. "Descriptivism", in W. D. Hudson (ed.), *The Is-Ought Question.* London: Macmillan, 1969, pp. 240–58.

———. "Wanting: Some Pitfalls" in Robert Binkley, Richard Bronaugh, and Ausonio Marras (eds.), *Agent, Action and Reason.* Toronto: University of Toronto Press, 1971, pp. 81–97.

——. "Imperative Sentences", pp. 1–21. "Meaning and Speech Acts", pp. 74–93. "Appendix: Reply to Mr. G. J. Warnock", pp. 94–99. "Austin's Distinction between Locutionary and Illocutionary Acts", pp. 100–14. In R.M. Hare, *Practical Inferences*. London: Macmillan, 1971.

——. Review of Hector-Neri Castañeda's *The Structure of Morality*, *Journal of Philosophy* 73 (1976): 481–485.

——. *Moral Thinking: Its Levels, Method and Point*. Oxford: Oxford University Press, 1981.

Harman, Gilbert. *Thought*. Princeton, N.J.: Princeton University Press, 1973.

——. "Practical Reasoning", *Review of Metaphysics* 29 (1975–76): 433–63.

——. *The Nature of Morality*. Oxford: Oxford University Press, 1977.

Harrison, Jonathan. "When Is a Principle a Moral Principle?" *Proceedings of the Aristotelian Society* Supp. Vol. 27 (1954): 111–34.

Hemingway, Ernest. *The Old Man and the Sea*. London: Jonathan Cape, 1962.

Hempel, Carl. *Aspects of Scientific Explanation*. New York: Free Press, 1965.

Holborow, Les. "The Commitment Fallacy", *Noûs* 5 (1971): 385–94.

——. Critical Notice of John R. Searle's *Speech Acts*, *Mind* 81 (1972): 458–68.

Holdcroft, David. *Words and Deeds: Problems in the Theory of Speech Acts*. Oxford: Oxford University Press, 1978.

Holmes, Robert L. "Is Morality a System of Hypothetical Imperatives?" *Analysis* 34 (1973–74): 96–100.

——. "Philippa Foot on Hypothetical Imperatives", *Analysis* 36 (1976–77): 199–200.

Horsburgh, H. J. N. "The Criteria of Assent to a Moral Rule", in Geoffrey Mortimore (ed.), *Weakness of Will*, pp. 118–31. London: Macmillan, 1971.

Hume, David. *A Treatise of Human Nature*. Edited by L. A. Selby-Bigge. Oxford: Oxford University Press, 1967.

Irwin, T. W. "Aristotle on Reason, Desire, and Virtue", *Journal of Philosophy* 72 (1975): 567–78.

Jarvis, Judith. "Practical Reasoning", *Philosophical Quarterly* 12 (1962): 316–28.

Kant, Immanuel. *Fundamental Principles of the Metaphysic of Morals*. Translated by Thomas K. Abbott. New York: Liberal Arts Press, 1949.

Kaufman, Arnold S. "Practical Decisions", *Mind* 75 (1966): 25–44.

Kemp, J. Review of R. M. Hare's *The Language of Morals, Philosophical Quarterly* 4 (1954): 94–96.

Kenny, Anthony. *Action, Emotion and Will.* London: Routledge and Kegan Paul, 1963.

——. "Oratio Obliqua", *Proceedings of the Aristotelian Society* Supp. Vol. 37 (1963): 126–46.

——. "Practical Inference", *Analysis* 26 (1966): 65–75.

——. "The Practical Syllogism and Incontinence", pp. 28–50. "Aristotle on Happiness", pp. 51–61. In Kenny, *The Anatomy of the Soul: Historical Essays in the Philosophy of Mind.* Oxford: Basil Blackwell, 1973.

——. *Will, Freedom and Power.* Oxford: Basil Blackwell, 1975.

——. *Aristotle's Theory of the Will.* London: Gerald Duckworth, 1979.

Kim, Jaegwon. "Intention and Practical Inference", in Juha Manninen and Raimo Tuomela (eds.), *Essays on Explanation and Understanding.* Dordrecht: D. Reidel, 1976, pp. 249–69.

Korner, S. *Kant.* Harmondsworth, Middlesex: Penguin Books, 1970.

Kubara, Michael. "Acrasia, Human Agency and Normative Psychology", *Canadian Journal of Philosophy* 5 (1975): 215–32.

Lawrence, D. H. *Love among the Haystacks and Other Stories.* Harmondsworth: Middlesex: Penguin Books, 1978.

Lemmon, E. J. "Moral Dilemmas", *Philosophical Review* 71 (1962): 139–58.

Locke, Don. "Reasons, Wants and Causes", *American Philosophical Quarterly* 11 (1974): 169–79.

Luckhardt, C. G. "Remorse, Regret and the Socratic Paradox", *Analysis* 35 (1975): 159–66.

Lukes, Stephen. "Moral Weakness", in Geoffrey Mortimore (ed.), *Weakness of Will.* London: Macmillan, 1971, pp. 147–59.

Mabbott, J. D. "Reason and Desire", *Philosophy* 28 (1953): 113–23.

McConnell, Terrance. "Is Aristotle's Account of Incontinence Inconsistent?" *Canadian Journal of Philosophy* 4 (1975): 635–751.

McDowell, John, and I. G. McFetridge. "Are Moral Requirements Hypothetical Imperatives?" *Proceedings of the Aristotelian Society* Supp. Vol. 52 (1978): 13–42.

McGuire, M. C. "Decisions, Resolutions and Moral Conduct", *Philosophical Quarterly* 11 (1961): 61–67.

——. "Can I Do What I Think I Ought Not? Where Has Hare Gone Wrong?" *Mind* 70 (1961): 400–404.

MacIntyre, Alasdair. "Imperatives, Reasons for Action, and Morals", *Journal of Philosophy* 62 (1965): 513–24.

——. *A Short History of Ethics*. London: Routledge and Kegan Paul, 1967.

Mackie, J. L. *Ethics: Inventing Right and Wrong*. Harmondsworth, Middlesex: Penguin Books, 1977.

McQueen, D. "Belief and Reasons for Belief", *Proceedings of the Aristotelian Society* Supp. Vol. 47 (1973): 69–86.

Margolis, Joseph. "Moral Utterances and Imperatives", *Journal of Philosophy* 62 (1965): 525–28.

——. "The Analysis of 'Ought' ", *Australasian Journal of Philosophy* 48 (1970): 44–53.

——. *Values and Conduct*. Oxford: Oxford University Press, 1971.

Matthews, Gwynneth. "Weakness of Will", in Geoffrey Mortimore (ed.), *Weakness of Will*. London: Macmillan, 1971, pp. 160–74.

Mayo, Bernard. "Varieties of Imperative", *Proceedings of the Aristotelian Society* Supp. Vol. 31 (1957): 161–74.

Meikle, Scott. "Reasons for Action", *Philosophical Quarterly* 24 (1974): 52–66.

Meiland, Jack W. *The Nature of Intention*. London: Methuen, 1970.

Melden, A. I. *Free Action*. London: Routledge and Kegan Paul, 1961.

——. "Expressives, Descriptives, Performatives", *Philosophy and Phenomenological Research* 29 (Sept. 1968–June 1969): 498–505.

Mill, John Stuart. "Utilitarianism", in Maurice Cowling (ed.), *Selected Writings of John Stuart Mill*. New York: New American Library, 1968, pp. 243–306.

Milton, John. *Paradise Lost*. In David Masson (ed.), *The Poetical Works of John Milton*. London: Macmillan, 1910.

Mitchell, Basil. "Varieties of Imperative", *Proceedings of the Aristotelian Society* Supp. Vol. 31 (1957): 175–90.

Montefiore, Alan. " 'Ought' and 'Can' ", *Philosophical Quarterly* 8 (1958): 24–40.

——. "Goodness and Choice", *Proceedings of the Aristotelian Society* Supp. Vol. 35 (1961): 61–80.

Mothersill, Mary. Review of R. M. Hare's *The Language of Morals*, *Journal of Philosophy* 51 (1954): 24–28.

Myers, G. E. "Motives and Wants", *Mind* 73 (1964): 173–85.

Nagel, Thomas. *The Possibility of Altruism*. Oxford: Oxford University Press, 1970.

Neblett, William. "Feelings of Obligation", *Mind* 85 (1976): 341–50.

Nesbitt, Winston. "Categorical Imperatives: A Defense", *Philosophical Review* 86 (1977): 217–25.

Norman, Richard. *Reasons for Actions*. Oxford: Basil Blackwell, 1971.

Norris, Stephen. "The Intelligibility of Practical Reasoning", *American Philosophical Quarterly* 12 (1975): 77–84.

Nowell-Smith, P. H. *Ethics*. Harmondsworth, Middlesex: Penguin Books, 1954.

O'Hear, Anthony. "Belief and the Will", *Philosophy* 47 (1972): 95–112.

Oldenquist, A. "Choosing, Deciding and Doing", in Paul Edwards (ed.), *The Encyclopedia of Philosophy* 2. New York: Macmillan, 1967, pp. 96–104.

Onions, C. T. *Modern English Syntax*. Revised Edition, by B. D. H. Miller. London: Routledge and Kegan Paul, 1971.

O'Shaughnessy, Brian. "The Limits of the Will", *Philosophical Review* 65 (1956): 443–90.

——. *The Will: A Dual Aspect Theory*. Cambridge: Cambridge University Press, 1980.

Parsons, Howard L. "Reason and Affect: Some of their Relations and Functions", *Journal of Philosophy* 55 (1958): 221–30.

Passmore, John A. "Intentions", *Proceedings of the Aristotelian Society* Supp. Vol. 29 (1955): 131–46.

Patton, Thomas B. and Paul Ziff. "On Vendler's Grammar of 'Good' ", *Philosophical Review* 73 (1964): 528–37.

Pears, David F. "Comments", in Robert Binkley, Richard Bronaugh, and Ausonio Marras (eds.), *Agent, Action and Reason*. Toronto: University of Toronto Press, 1971.

——. "Predicting and Deciding", pp. 13–38. "Sketch for a Causal Theory of Wanting and Doing", pp. 97–141. In Pears, *Questions in the Philosophy of Mind*. London: Gerald Duckworth, 1975.

——. "Motivated Irrationality, Freudian Theory and Cognitive Dissonance", in Richard Wollheim and James Hopkins (eds.), *Philosophical Essays on Freud*. Cambridge: Cambridge University Press, 1982, pp. 264–88.

Penner, Terry. "Thought and Desire in Plato", in Gregory Vlastos (ed.), *Plato: A Collection of Critical Essays*. Vol. 2, *Ethics, Politics, and Philosophy of Art and Religion.* Garden City, N.Y.: Doubleday Anchor, 1971, pp. 96–118.

Perry, R. B. "Value and Its Moving Appeal", *Philosophical Review* 41 (1932): 337–50.

Peters, A. F. "R. M. Hare on Imperative Sentences: A Criticism", *Mind* 58 (1949): 535–40.

Peters, R. S. "Motives and Motivation", *Philosophy* 31 (1956): 117–30.

———. *The Concept of Motivation.* 2d Ed. London: Routledge and Kegan Paul, 1960.

Phillips, D. Z. "In Search of the Moral 'Must': Mrs. Foot's Fugitive Thought", *Philosophical Quarterly* 27 (1977): 140–57.

———, and H. O. Mounce. "On Morality's Having a Point", in W. D. Hudson (ed.), *The Is-Ought Question.* London: Macmillan, 1969, pp. 228–39.

———, and W. S. Price. "Remorse without Repudiation", *Analysis* 28 (1967–68): 18–20.

Phillips Griffiths, A. "Acting with Reason", in Geoffrey Mortimore (ed.), *Weakness of Will.* London: Macmillan, 1971, pp. 177–89.

———. "Belief and Reason for Belief", *Proceedings of the Aristotelian Society* Supp. Vol. 67 (1973): 53–68.

Pole, David. "Virtue and Reason", *Proceedings of the Aristotelian Society* Supp. Vol. 68 (1974): 43–62.

Plato. *The Symposium.* Translated by Walter Hamilton. Harmondsworth, Middlesex: Penguin Books, 1951.

———. *The Republic.* Translated by H. D. P. Lee. Harmondsworth, Middlesex: Penguin Books, 1955.

———. *Protagoras* and *Meno.* Translated by W. K. C. Guthrie. Harmondsworth, Middlesex: Penguin Books, 1956.

Price, H. H. "Belief and Will", *Proceedings of the Aristotelian Society* Supp. Vol. 28 (1954): 1–26.

Price, Richard. "Review of the Principal Questions in Morals", in L. A. Selby-Bigge (ed.), *British Moralists* II. Oxford: Oxford University Press, 1897, pp. 105–84.

Rachels, James. "Wanting and Willing", *Philosophical Studies* 20 (1969): 9–13.

———. "Reasons for Action", *Canadian Journal of Philosophy* 1 (1971): 173–87.

Rapaport, Elizabeth. "Explaining Moral Weakness", *Philosophical Studies* 24 (1973): 174–82.

——. "Describing Moral Weakness", *Philosophical Studies* 28 (1975): 273–80.

Raz, Joseph "Reasons for Action, Decisions and Norms", *Mind* 84 (1975): 481–99.

Reba, Marilyn. "A Second Look at Nagel's Argument for Altruism", *Philosophical Studies* 25 (1974): 429–34.

Rescher, Nicholas. *The Logic of Commands.* London: Routledge and Kegan Paul; New York: Dover, 1966.

Richards, David A. J. *A Theory of Reasons for Action.* Oxford: Oxford University Press, 1971.

Richards, Norvin W. "Acting for Reasons", *Philosophical Studies* 26 (1974): 135–39.

Robinson, Richard. "Ought and Ought Not", *Philosophy* 46 (1971): 193–202.

Rorty, Amelie. "Wants and Justifications", *Journal of Philosophy* 62 (1966): 765–72.

——. "Plato and Aristotle on Belief, Habit, and *Akrasia*", *American Philosophical Quarterly* 7 (1970): 50–61.

——. "Belief and Self-deception", *Inquiry* 15 (1972): 387–410.

——. "Where Does the Akratic Break Take Place?" *Australasian Journal of Philosophy* 58 (1980): 333–46.

Ross, W. D. *The Right and the Good.* Oxford: Oxford University Press, 1930.

——. *Foundations of Ethics.* Oxford: Oxford University Press, 1939.

——. *Aristotle.* London: Methuen, 1964.

Santas, Gerasimos. "The Socratic Paradoxes", *Philosophical Review* 73 (1964): 147–64.

——. "Plato's *Protagoras* and Explanations of Weakness", in Geoffrey Mortimore (ed.), *Weakness of Will.* London: Macmillan, 1971, pp. 37–62.

Scheuler, G. F. "Nagel on the Rationality of Prudence", *Philosophical Studies* 29 (1976): 69–73.

Schiffer, Stephen. "A Paradox of Desire", *American Philosophical Quarterly* 13 (1976): 195–208.

Scott, Stephen. "Practical Reason and the Concept of a Human Being", *Journal of Philosophy* 73 (1976): 497–510.

Scott-Taggart, A. J. "Comment: 'Kant, Conduct and Consistency' ", in Stephen Korner (ed.), *Practical Reason*. Oxford: Basil Blackwell, 1974, pp. 221–57.

Searle, John R. "Meaning and Speech Acts", pp. 28–37. "Rejoinder", pp. 50–54. In C. D. Rollins (ed.), *Knowledge and Experience*. Pittsburgh: University of Pittsburg Press, 1966.

——. "Austin on Locutionary and Illocutionary Acts", *Philosophical Review* 77 (1968): 405–24.

——. *Speech Acts*. Cambridge: Cambridge University Press, 1970.

——. "Indirect Speech Acts", in Peter Cole and Jerry L. Morgan (eds.), *Syntax and Semantics: Speech Acts 3*. London: Academic Press, 1975, pp. 59–82.

——. "A Classification of Illocutionary Acts", *Language in Society* 5 (1976): 1–23.

——. *Expression and Meaning: Studies in the Theory of Speech Acts*. Cambridge: Cambridge University Press, 1979.

Sellars, Wilfred. "Obligation and Motivation", in Sellars and John Hospers (eds.), *Readings in Ethical Theory*. New York: Appleton-Century-Crofts, 1952, pp. 511–17.

——. "Imperatives, Intentions and the Logic of 'Ought' ", in Hector-Neri Castañeda and George Nakhnikian (eds.), *Morality and the Language of Conduct*, pp. 158–218. Detroit: Wayne State University Press, 1963.

——. "Belief and the Expression of Belief", in Howard Kiefer and Milton K. Munitz (eds.), *Language, Belief and Metaphysics*. Albany: State University of New York Press, 1970, pp. 146–59.

Sesonske, Alexander. *Value and Obligation*. New York: Oxford University Press, 1964.

Shorey, Paul. "Plato's Ethics", in Gregory Vlastos (ed.), *Plato, A Collection of Critical Essays*. Vol. 2, *Ethics, Politics, and Philosophy of Art and Religion*. Garden City, N.Y.: Doubleday Anchor, 1971, pp. 7–34.

Shwayder, D. S. "The Sense of Duty", *Philosophical Quarterly* 7 (1957): 116–25.

——. *The Stratification of Behaviour*. London: Routledge and Kegan Paul, 1965.

Sidorsky, David. "A Note on Three Criticisms of Von Wright", *Journal of Philosophy* 62 (1965): 739–42.

Silverstein, Harry S. "Prescriptivism and Akrasia", *Philosophical Studies* 21 (1970): 81–85.

Singer, Marcus G. "Moral Rules and Principles", in A. I. Melden (ed.), *Essays in Moral Philosophy*. Seattle: University of Washington Press, 1956, pp. 160–97.

Sloman, Aaron. " 'Ought' and 'Better' ", *Mind* 79 (1970): 385–94.

Smythe, Thomas W. "Unconscious Desires and the Meaning of 'Desires' ", *Monist* 56 (1972): 413–25.

Snare, Frank. "The Argument from Motivation", *Mind* 84 (1975): 1–9.

Solomon, William David. "Moral Reasons", *American Philosophical Quarterly* 12 (1975): 331–39.

Stevenson, C. L. "The Emotive Meaning of Ethical Terms", in Joseph Margolis (ed.), *Contemporary Ethical Theory*. New York: Random House, 1966, pp. 81–103.

Stocker, Michael. "Desiring the Bad: An Essay in Moral Psychology", *Journal of Philosophy* 76 (1979): 738–53.

Sturgeon, Nicholas L. "Altruism, Solipsism, and the Objectivity of Reasons", *Philosophical Review* 83 (1974): 374–402.

Sullivan, Roger J. "The Kantian Critique of Aristotle's Moral Philosophy: An Appraisal", *Review of Metaphysics* 28 (1974): 24–53.

Taylor, C. C. W. Review of R. M. Hare's *Freedom and Reason*, *Mind* 74 (1965): 280–98.

Taylor, Charles. *The Explanation of Behaviour*. London: Routledge and Kegan Paul, 1964.

———. "Explaining Action", *Inquiry* 13 (1970): 54–89.

Taylor, Richard. *Action and Purpose*. Englewood Cliffs, N.J.: Prentice-Hall, 1966.

Thalberg, Irving. "Remorse", *Mind* 72 (1963): 545–55.

———. "Acting against One's Better Judgement", in Geoffrey Mortimore (ed.), *Weakness of Will*. London: Macmillan, 1971, pp. 233–46.

———. "Constituents and Causes of Emotion and Action", *Philosophical Quarterly* 23 (1973): 1–14.

Tomás, Vincent. Review of R. M. Hare's *The Language of Morals*, *Philosophical Review* 64 (1955): 132–35.

Toulmin, Stephen E. *The Uses of Argument.* Cambridge: Cambridge University Press, 1958.

Tuomela, Raimo. "Explanation and Understanding of Behavior", in Juha Manninen and Toumela (eds.), *Essays on Explanation and Understanding.* Dordrecht: D. Reidel, 1976, pp. 183–205.

Turnbull, Robert G. "Imperatives, Logic, and Moral Obligation", *Philosophy of Science* 27 (1960): 374–90.

Urmson, J. O. "On Grading" in Antony Flew (ed.), *Logic and Language.* 2d Series. Oxford: Basil Blackwell, 1973, pp. 159–86.

Valberg, J. J. "Some Remarks on Action and Desire", *Journal of Philosophy* 67 (1970): 503–20.

Vendler, Zeno. "Comments", in C. D. Rollins (ed.), *Knowledge and Experience.* Pittsburgh: University of Pittsburgh Press, 1966, pp. 38–42.

——. "The Grammar of Goodness", in Vendler, *Linguistics in Philosophy.* Ithaca, N.Y.: Cornell University Press, 1967, pp. 172–95.

——. *Adjectives and Nominalizations.* The Hague: Mouton, 1968.

——. *Res Cogitans.* Ithaca, N.Y.: Cornell University Press, 1972.

Von Wright, Georg Henrik. *Norm and Action.* London: Routledge and Kegan Paul, 1963.

——. *The Varieties of Goodness.* London: Routledge and Kegan Paul, 1963.

——. "Practical Inference", *Philosophical Review* 72 (1963): 159–79.

——. *Explanation and Understanding.* London: Routledge and Kegan Paul, 1971.

——. "On So-Called Practical Inference", *Acta Sociologica* 15 (1972): 39–53.

——. "Replies", in Juha Manninen and Raimo Tuomela (eds.), *Essays on Explanation and Understanding.* Dordrecht: D. Reidel, 1976, pp. 371–413.

Walsh, James J. "Remarks on *Thought and Action*", *Journal of Philosophy* 60 (1963): 57–65.

Walsh, W. H. "Kant's Concept of Practical Reason", in Stephen Korner (ed.), *Practical Reason.* Oxford: Basil Blackwell, 1974, pp. 189–212.

Walton, K. A. "Rational Action", *Mind* 76 (1967): 537–47.

Warnock, G. J. *Contemporary Moral Philosophy.* London: Macmillan, 1967.

——. "Hare on Meaning and Speech Acts", *Philosophical Review* 80 (1971): 80–84.

——. *The Object of Morality.* London: Methuen, 1971.

Warnock, Mary. *Ethics since 1900.* 2d Ed. Oxford: Oxford University Press, 1966.

Watson, Gary. ''Skepticism about Weakness of Will'', *Philosophical Review* 86 (1977): 316–39.

Wedeking, Gary A. ''Reasons for Acting versus Reasons for Believing'', *Analysis* 33 (1972–73): 102–6.

Wertheimer, Roger. *The Significance of Sense: Meaning and Morality.* Ithaca, N.Y.: Cornell University Press, 1972.

White, Alan R. ''Inclination'', *Analysis* 21 (1960–61): 40–42.

——. *The Philosophy of Mind.* New York: Random House, 1967.

——. *Modal Thinking.* Ithaca, N. Y.: Cornell University Press, 1975.

Wiggins, David. ''Weakness of Will, Commensurability, and the Objects of Deliberation and Desire'', *Proceedings of the Aristotelian Society* 79 (1978–79): 251–77.

Williams, Bernard. ''Ethical Consistency'', pp. 166–86. ''Morality and the Emotions'', pp. 207–29. ''Egoism and Altruism'', pp. 250–65. In Williams (ed.), *Problems of the Self.* Cambridge: Cambridge University Press, 1973.

Wittgenstein, Ludwig. *Philosophical Investigations.* Translated by G. E. M. Anscombe. Oxford: Basil Blackwell, 1953.

——. *Zettel.* Edited by G. E. M. Anscombe and G. H. von Wright. Oxford: Basil Blackwell, 1967.

Woods, Michael. ''Reasons for Action and Desires'', *Proceedings of the Aristotelian Society* Supp. Vol. 46 (1972): 189–201.

Wright, Derek. *The Psychology of Moral Behaviour.* Harmondsworth, Middlesex: Penguin Books, 1971.

Young, Robert. ''Autonomy and the 'Inner Self' '', *American Philosophical Quarterly* 17 (1980): 35–43.

Zimmerman, David. ''Force and Sense'', *Mind* 89 (1980): 214–33.

Index

Index includes explanatory notes

also, 137n23
see also commending
evaluative sentences
    and conative sentences, 16–17, 57, 78–80
    and imperatives, 6–8, 15–17, 28–56, 78
    and indicatives, 15–17, 18, 19, 85, 148n16
    and intentives, 16–17, 78–80
evaluative terms
    and being of value, 19–20, 85–100
    in conditional clauses, 36–39
    and imperative mood-signs, 6, 29–31, 39, 44, 50–55 passim
    prescriptivist analysis of, 6, 28–30, 33–39, 52–55, 136n12
    and concept of reason, 19–20, 85–86, 97–99
    univocality of, 33–39, 52–55, 80–81, 136n12
    see also good; ought; right
evaluative thinking, all-out
    action contrary to, 1–13 passim, 124–25
    and ahi thinking, 18–21, 84–85, 99–100, 101–23, 125
    and all-things-considered evaluation, 10–13, 14
    and cognitive thinking, 15–17 passim, 21, 28, 39, 57, 77, 81, 83, 84, 148n16
    felicitous, 18, 83–84
    and reasons for acting, 19–21, 83–100, 146n8
    connection with volitional thinking, 1–3, 5–8, 10, 124–25
        as intrinsic, 13–17, 28–82, 83–85, 124
        as extrinsic, 18–27, 83–125
    also, 126n1, 137n23
Ewing, A. C., 95
expressive illocutions, 40–44, 137n21, 137n22

felicitous evaluation, 18, 83–84
Foot, Philippa, 101–103
Fowler, H. W., 67
Freud, Sigmund, 128n28

Gauthier, David, 76
Geach, Peter, 38, 137n22, 141n18
good
    and being of value, 19–20, 85–91, 97
    and commending, 29–30, 33–44 passim
    in conditional clauses, 36–39